BLUNDERS IN INTERNATIONAL
BUSINESS

D0395188

To

Artel and Focha Ricks

Woodrow and Barbara Williams

BLUNDERS IN INTERNATIONAL BUSINESS

David A. Ricks

Thunderbird
American Graduate School of International Management

First published 1993
Blackwell Publishers
238 Main Street
Cambridge, Massachusetts 02142
USA

108 Cowley Road
Oxford OX4 1JF
UK

Library of Congress Cataloging-in-Publication Data

Ricks, David A.
    Blunders in international business / David A. Ricks.
      p. cm.
    Includes bibliographical references and index.
    ISBN 1-55786-414-4
    1. International business enterprises—Management—Case studies.
  2. Business failures—Case studies.   I. Title.
    HD62.4.R53   1993
    658'.049—dc20   92-33483
                                                         CIP

CONTENTS

PREFACE

We often hear of business success stories. It seems that everyone is willing to relate past successes. However, unless these tales are absolutely incredible, we tend to forget them and consequently learn little of value.

Mistakes, on the other hand, are seldom admitted, are easily remembered, and can be used to illustrate valuable lessons. In fact, I began this collection of international business blunders when I discovered how effectively they could be used in the classroom. One day, after discussing what many of my students thought was a minor point related to international business, I cited a few blunders made by firms that had overlooked the concept under discussion. The students thoroughly enjoyed the blunders – so much so that not only did they remember the concepts but they wanted to learn more about international business.

As I encountered more reported blunders, I incorporated them into my classroom lectures with similar results and began to realize that I had stumbled onto a useful and enjoyable teaching tool. At this point, I decided to search seriously for blunders committed by multinational corporations. With the assistance of Professor Jeffrey S. Arpan, University of South Carolina; Marilyn Y. C. Fu Harpster, a former Ohio State graduate student; and Professor Donald Patton, Dalhousie

University, I corresponded with those teaching international business and scoured the journals and business periodicals searching for blunders. We published a few articles, and in 1974 wrote a book called *International Business Blunders*, which was published by Grid, Inc.

The book was favorably reviewed in *Business Week* and *Forbes,* and was also well received within the academic community. As I continued to gather reports of new or different blunders, the collection grew and gained the attention of the news media. As the public became aware of my collection, individuals began to send me evidence of even more blunders. All of this eventually led to suggestions that I write about the cases in multinational marketing I had uncovered.

I did so and the book, *Big Business Blunders: Mistakes in Multinational Marketing*, was published in 1983 by Richard D. Irwin, Inc. The book sold well to both the trade and the academic communities. However, it did not contain many of the nonmarketing blunders I had uncovered.

Since 1983 I have learned of many more blunders that have occurred in all areas of international business. I now welcome the opportunity to share my collection with you because I truly believe that we can learn from the mistakes of others. Of course, it is not the only learning method, but it is an interesting and enjoyable one and surely preferable to learning through experience.

Many individuals have aided me in the collection and presentation of these blunders. My wife, Lesley, deserves the most credit. Not only has she been patient and supportive, but she has literally served as an editor and critic. My former co-authors – Jeffrey S. Arpan, Marilyn Harpster, Donald Patton, and Vijay Mahajan – were tremendous in their encouragement and assistance in previous research efforts. I especially appreciate their understanding and tolerance of my continuing interest in these blunders. Kari Morgenthaler, a master's student at Thunderbird, the American Graduate School of International Management; Peter Bemelman, Katherine Huelster, Martin Meznar, and Pedro Sanabria, graduate students in international business at the University of South Carolina; and former Ohio State University student Jeff Sugheir have aided by serving as research assistants. Dina Forsythe deserves credit for her efficient secretarial services. Several other people have been of assistance by sending me information about business blunders. To all these people, I wish to express my sincere appreciation.

David A. Ricks

1
INTRODUCTION

International business is fraught with unexpected events. Fortunately, some of these surprising occurrences prove to be advantageous to the multinational companies involved. For example, a U.S. firm selling feminine sanitary napkins in South America suddenly experienced a major surge in sales. The company was delighted, although a bit startled, when it discovered that the sales boost was prompted by local farmers buying the napkins to use as dust masks. No less surprised was a U.S. company that sold toothbrushes in South Vietnam during the late 1960s. It too experienced an unexpected increase in sales. Years later the company learned why: The Vietcong had purchased the toothbrushes to use for weapon cleaning.

Other firms have also encountered unexpected product marketability as a result of unplanned and often unimagined uses for their products. These surprises, although sometimes controversial, are normally welcomed by the "lucky" companies. However, not all firms experience such good fortune. In fact, many surprises in international business are quite undesirable.

Sometimes companies are caught off guard by an unavoidable turn of events. Other times, though, they are unhappily surprised by outcomes that they could have avoided. A company is said to have "blundered" if it makes a decision resulting in a costly or embarrassing situation that was foreseeable and avoidable.

The foreign environment has been especially difficult for some to analyze. Many mistakes, for example, have been made because managers have failed to remember that consumers differ from country to country. Buyers, influenced by local economic constraints and by local values, attitudes, and tastes, differ in what they buy, why they buy, how they buy, when they buy, and where they buy. Managers who have failed to recognize these differences have committed a number of blunders.

THE ROLE OF CULTURE

Cultural differences are the most significant and troublesome variables encountered by the multinational company. The failure of managers to comprehend fully these disparities has led to most international business blunders. A European businessman, for example, while on an important negotiating trip to China, playfully flipped a piece of ice from his drink towards his companion. Unluckily for him, the ice accidentally landed on a nearby official and the businessman was soon sent packing. Another unlucky individual found himself home sooner than expected after he flippantly patted a waitress. The Chinese simply do not accept such foolishness, as many a playful visitor can attest.

In 1983 Columbia Pictures produced a four-hour movie set in Egypt that resulted in the banning of all Columbia Pictures in Egypt. The Egyptian authorities were offended by the numerous inaccuracies that included accent (Pakistani), clothing (Moroccan), and behavior (American). The late

Egyptian president Gamal Abdel Nasser, for example, was portrayed publicly kissing his wife – an unacceptable act in Egypt and in many other countries.

During the groundbreaking ceremonies for Hitachi Ltd's subsidiary, Hitachi Automotive Products (USA), Inc., the Governor of Kentucky presented the Japanese executives with a flag of the Commonwealth of Kentucky. After opening the flag for all to see, the Japanese carelessly dragged it along the ground. In Japan (and in many other countries), flags are not treated with the same respect as they are in America. The Japanese really meant no disrespect; they simply were unaware of American customs about flags. However, many in the audience, especially the older Americans, were offended.

We all know that some things are done differently by the peoples of other countries, but sometimes these differences are hard to embrace. Consider, for instance, what happened when a man from Tonga answered a neighbor's ad in a Salt Lake City newspaper. The neighbor wanted to sell his son's pony. When the neighbor asked the Tongan why he wanted to purchase the pony, the Tongan replied that he wanted it for his own son's birthday. The seller was satisfied with the reply so the deal was closed. Then before the seller's eyes, the Tongan casually turned, picked up a board, and clubbed the pony to death. The dead pony was tossed into the Tongan's truck and hauled home. When the police arrived, they found a huge birthday party in progress with many Tongans happily cooking the pony for a typical Tongan birthday dinner.

All nationalities possess unique characteristics that must be understood. For example, Arabs typically dislike deadlines. An Arab faced with a deadline tends to feel threatened and backed into a corner. Many Americans, on the other hand, try to expedite matters by setting deadlines. As a result, hundreds of

American-owned radio sets are sitting untouched in Middle Eastern repair shops because some Americans made the cultural mistake of requesting that the work be completed by a certain time.

American business managers have encountered similar problems trying to understand time values in other cultures. One U.S. company lost a major contract opportunity in Greece because its managers tried to impose American customs on the Greek negotiators. Besides being too forthright and outspoken in the eyes of the Greeks, the Americans tried to set time limits for the meetings. The Greeks, however, considered time limits insulting and thus felt that the Americans showed a lack of finesse. The Americans also wanted the Greeks to first agree to principles, and then allow their subordinates to work out all necessary details. The Greeks viewed this as a deceptive strategy; they preferred to directly handle all arrangements regardless of the time involved.[1]

In France, McDonald's overlooked a cultural difference that led to years of litigation. In selecting a French partner, McDonald's examined a number of characteristics that would ensure sales. McDonald's is very good at this and, as usual, was successful. However, it did not examine carefully enough its partner's attitudes about cleanliness. Because French firms place less emphasis on cleanliness than American firms do, local references of the French partner did not expose this as a potential problem. As business in France grew, however, McDonald's soon observed hygiene habits it considered unacceptable in its U.S. outlets. These habits, though, were not viewed as negatively by the French partner or by most of the French customers, for that matter. The real problem? Many of the outlets' customers were American tourists expecting American standards. The French outlets, therefore, negatively affected McDonald's global image and threatened its "clean" reputation at home.

In the United States, a local supermarket hoping to impress Japanese visitors served sushi and tea to its guests. Unfortunately, not only did it serve the fish cooked when the fish should have been served raw, but the supermarket also served *Chinese* tea.

Such failures to understand cultural differences can bear serious consequences. Consider an unfortunate American manager who worked in the South Pacific. He foolishly hired local natives without considering the island's traditional status system. By hiring too many of one group, he threatened to alter the balance of power of the people. The islanders discussed this unacceptable situation and independently developed an alternative plan. It had taken them until 3:00 a.m. to do so, however. But since time was not important in their culture, they saw no reason to wait until morning to present their suggestions to the American. They casually went to his place of residence, but their arrival at such a late hour caused him to panic. Since he could not understand their language and could not imagine that they would want to discuss business at 3:00 a.m., he assumed that they were coming to riot and called in the Marines. It was some time before the company was able to get back to business as usual.

Knowing what to do is as important as knowing what *not* to do. In India, for instance, it is considered a violation of sacred hospitality mores to discuss business in the home or on social occasions. And if a business executive from India offers "come any time," it is an honest invitation and not just a polite expression as often used in the United States. The Indian is requesting a visit but is politely allowing the guest to arrange the time of the meeting. If no time is set, the Indian will assume that the invitation has been refused. The failure to understand this local custom has led to some serious misunderstandings.

Even the rejection of a cup of coffee can cause major problems. While a very profitable opportunity was being negotiated, one U.S. executive innocently made the mistake of refusing a Saudi Arabian's friendly offer to join him for a cup of coffee. Such a rejection is considered an affront in Saudi Arabia. Naturally, the Saudi became much less sociable, and the negotiation process was far less successful than it might have been.

Gift giving can also create troubles. Sometimes gifts are expected and the failure to supply them is seen as insulting. Other times, however, the mere offer of such a token is considered offensive. In the Middle East, for example, hosts are insulted if guests bring food or drink to their homes because they believe that such gifts imply that they are not good hosts. (Liquor, of course, is an especially dangerous gift because it is prohibited by the Islamic religion.) In many parts of Latin America, cutlery or handkerchiefs should not be given because these gifts imply the cutting off of a relationship or the likelihood of a tearful event. And giving a clock to someone in China is not a good idea, either. The Chinese word for clock sounds similar to their word for funeral. In fact, even the way in which a gift is presented is important. In most parts of Asia gifts should be given privately to avoid embarrassing the Asians, but in the Middle East they need to be offered publicly in order to avoid giving the impression that bribery is being attempted.[2]

To avoid making blunders, a person must be able to discern the difference between what must be done, what must not be done, and what may or may not be done. For example, shoes must be removed before entering many of the religious buildings of the world, but the individuals doing so must not act as if they are of the religion if, in fact, they are not.

Complete knowledge and understanding of a foreign culture, however, is almost impossible to acquire. In fact, no general agreement even exists as to what "culture" is, but most experts do concur that it is a complex set of variables involving a group's beliefs and ways of living. They also agree that an understanding of any foreign culture requires knowledge in a great many areas. Unfortunately, even a well-intentioned person can commit a blunder by overlooking just one seemingly unimportant aspect of a foreign culture.

THE ROLE OF COMMUNICATION

As stated, culture plays an important role in international business. Of all of the aspects of culture, communication may be the most critical and certainly has been involved in numerous blunders. Good communication linkages must be established between a company and its customers, its suppliers, its employees, and its host governments. Poor communication networks can and have caused difficulties.

Because so many potential communication barriers exist, it is especially difficult for companies to effectively communicate with potential buyers. Messages can be translated incorrectly, inappropriate media used, regulations overlooked, and economic or taste differences ignored. Sometimes the potential customer never receives the company's message, and at other times the message arrives but is of little value due to its ineffectiveness. Every once in a while the buyer receives the message, but to the company's dismay, the message sent was incorrect.

For example, it certainly would not be wise to say "yeah" to the Japanese. Not wise, that is, unless one wants to say "no" because "yeah" sounds like the Japanese word for "no." However, saying "so" should cause no problems since it means the same in both languages. (In China, by the way, the expression *boo-shih* means "not true." Americans have a remarkably similar-sounding phrase they sometimes use to imply that they don't believe something!)

Multinational companies are not the only entities vulnerable to communication problems, of course. Former President Jimmy Carter's speech in Poland will long be remembered for his incorrectly translated appreciation of the Polish women (whom his translator said he "lusted for"). Other well-known people have mangled public introductions by using incorrect titles and names. It seems that if there is a way to say something incorrectly, some poor soul has managed to do so.

Communication problems are not necessarily verbal. Nonverbal communication difficulties have also led to serious blunders. Nonverbal communication exists in many forms. Some kinds are intended to supplement verbal communication; others are used when verbal communication is not possible.

A true anecdote about an American couple touring Asia might best illustrate the risks involved when relying on nonverbal forms of expression while in a foreign environment. A wealthy couple, accompanied by their pet poodle, was enjoying a lengthy cruise around the world. At one of the ship's Asian stops, the couple, with their inseparable pet, decided to see the town's sights. After a lengthy walk, they chose to dine at a pleasant looking restaurant. Since the restaurant employees could not speak English and the tourists could speak no other language, they ordered their meals by pointing to various items on the menu. Knowing that the poodle was also hungry, the couple tried to order food for it. For a long time the waiter had a difficult time understanding, but after several attempts he seemed to have figured it all out. He pointed to the dog and then pointed to the kitchen. The couple interpreted this to mean that their pet could not eat in the dining area but must eat in the kitchen where the waiter had some food for it. They therefore agreed to let the waiter take the dog to the kitchen. After waiting a particularly long time, the waiter and the full staff proudly entered with the couple's order. One can imagine the tourists' horror when the chef lifted one of the lids to display how well he had cooked the poodle!

Misunderstandings and blunders have resulted from the misinterpretation of many forms of nonverbal communication. The old proverb, for instance, that "patience is a virtue" is all too often forgotten by Americans. On many occasions, this lapse of memory has led them to react inappropriately by trying to correct a situation rather than remaining patient. The "improper" amount of touching or eye contact has left many people feeling so uncomfortable that effective communication efforts have been hampered. Similarly, the "incorrect" distance between individuals engaged in conversation has led to the false conclusion that the other person is too aggressive and hostile or too cold and distrustful.

The people of each culture uniquely utilize body movements as methods of communication. The meanings of motions and signs common in one culture may relay something quite different in another. Consider, for example, the OK hand sign commonly used in the United States. In France it signifies zero, and in Japan it symbolizes money. In parts of South America, however, it is a vulgar gesture. One unfortunate company learned this when it had an entire catalog printed with an OK stamp on each page. Although the error was quickly discovered, it created a costly six-month delay while all the catalogs were reprinted.

Headshakes are particularly difficult to interpret. People in the United States shake their heads up and down to signify "yes." Many British, however, make the same motions just to indicate that they hear – not necessarily that they agree. To say "no," people shake their heads from side to side in the United States, jerk their heads back in a haughty manner in the Middle East, wave a hand in front of the face in the Far East, and shake a finger from side to side in Ethiopia.

To indicate interest, Asian Indians sometimes shift their heads from side to side in a slightly jerky manner. However, in New Zealand people suck in a bit of air to show the same interest. The U.S. gesture to slit one's throat means "I love you" in Swaziland. A backward victory symbol is an insulting gesture in Europe. Using a palm-up hand with moving index finger connotes "come here" in many countries but is considered vulgar in others. In Ethiopia, one beckons another by holding out the hand, palm down, and repeatedly closing the hand. The act of folding one's arms denotes respect in Fiji but indicates arrogance in Finland. To an Ethiopian, one finger to the lips requests silence from a child whereas four fingers to the lips are necessary to ask the same from an adult.

Pointing a finger is a dangerous action. In North America it is a very normal gesture, but it is considered very rude in many other parts of the world – especially in areas of Asia and Africa. It is usually much safer to merely close the hand and point with the thumb. However, even though pointing the thumb up is an easily recognized positive gesture in North America, that same thumbs-up signal is a vulgar insult in the Middle East.

Many cultures also have their own form of greeting. Often it is some variation of a handshake, but people also greet each other with hugs, nose rubs, kisses, and other gestures depending on the culture. Failure to be aware of these customs has led to awkward and embarrassing encounters and to serious misunderstandings.

Other forms of communication have also caused problems. Tone of voice, for example, can be important. Some cultures permit people to raise their voices when they are distant from one another, but loudness in other cultures is often associated with anger or a loss of self-control. Even laughter is interpreted differently around the world. While most countries consider it an expression of joy, some cultures discourage it. In many West African countries, laughter indicates embarrassment, discomfort, or surprise.

Ignorance of such differences in verbal and nonverbal forms of communication has resulted in many social and business blunders. Local people tend to be willing to overlook most of the mistakes tourists make; after all, they are just temporary visitors. Locals are much less tolerant of the errors of business people, especially those who represent firms trying to project an impression of permanent interest in the local economy. The consequences of erring, therefore, are much greater for businesses.

STRUCTURE

Some of the blunders that companies have committed while trying to engage in business in foreign countries are described and discussed in this book. Most of these blunders have been reported in the media, but only in small numbers at any one time and in no clear patterns. The gathering of hundreds of these reports provided an opportunity to group these blunders and to arrive at some universally applicable conclusions.

The blunders have been grouped into seven categories: production, names, marketing, translation, management, strategy, and "other." Production blunders – especially those related to building plants on inappropriate sites – have generally proven to be the most costly. Plant location and plant layout errors as well as mistakes involving products and packages are reported in the next chapter.

As pointed out in chapter 3, inappropriate product and company names have caused company headaches. On occasion, a company has introduced an old, established name in a country that misunderstands it. In other instances, a firm has created a new name, only to later regret its decision. Sometimes harmless and amusing, these blunders have at other times proven insulting, embarrassing, and costly.

Marketing mistakes are described in chapter 4. Communication problems, poor promotional strategies, and cultural differences have all played a part in the development of major marketing blunders. These types of errors are identified and discussed.

The highest percentage of blunders has been due to faulty translations. In fact, the number of translation errors is so vast that these errors are reported in a separate chapter, chapter 5. Carelessness, unexpected additional meanings, and improper use of idioms have all contributed to translation blunders.

Managerial blunders were generally caused because people did not understand or were not aware of cultural differences. Some people simply are not culturally sensitive enough to handle international assignments with success. Others may be sensitive but uniformed. A number of the management problems reported in chapter 6 were caused by management's lack of knowledge concerning local labor practices. These misunderstandings have often led to the most confrontational of all the reported incidents.

Strategic blunders are usually the most complex. They are also among the most difficult to overcome. Problems arising from companies' entry modes, their establishment of various alliances, and their planning of supply arrangements are discussed in chapter 7.

Multinational enterprises have also been involved in many other blunders. Chapter 8 details legal, financial, and market research blunders. These types of blunders are not as easy to uncover and rarely make headlines, but they can be just as costly. In fact, the chapter helps make it clear that a blunder can occur in any area of international business.

The final chapter explains what can be learned from the international business blunders reported in the book and provides some important, basic conclusions. Some final comments and observations are also outlined in chapter 9. Please note that this book was not written with the intent to poke fun at companies. Nor should anyone conclude that firms are constantly making foolish mistakes. Their overall record is good, but hopefully this book will help make the future record even better.

2
PRODUCTION

A great deal of attention has been focused recently on the service industries. They have certainly grown in importance, so it is easy to overlook the significance of other industries – ones that actually produce physical products. The production of physical products, however, is a vital part of international business.

Companies that manufacture physical products encounter their own unique set of risks and make blunders that firms in the service industries avoid. These blunders can involve the location or layout of the production activity, the product, or its package.

LOCATION/LAYOUT

China was recently forced to cancel a $5 billion contract it had negotiated with several Western companies because it miscalculated its needs and abilities. The plan for building the giant Baoshan Iron and Steel Works near Shanghai was doomed from the start. Negotiators on both sides failed to recognize that there were inadequate port, transportation, and power facilities in the area, and an additional $9 billion would have been required to develop these needed facilities. Furthermore, the oil revenues that the planners had projected to generate the original $5 billion needed fell far short of expectations. China lost face, and its jilted Western partners lost confidence in China.

Others have experienced similar problems. In 1967 one of Daniel Ludwig's firms cleared huge tracts of Amazonian land. Unfortunately, the company belatedly discovered that the soil was inadequate for growing the kinds of trees it wished to grow.

A well-known multinational fiber producer, Celanese, purchased a large tract of land containing eucalyptus trees in Sicily. It planned to build a pulp processing plant and then use the local trees as raw material. It was not until the plant was built and production was to begin that the company discovered that the local trees were too small, the supply too limited, and the logs unsuitable for use. The result: The firm was forced to import pulp at a cost so high the plant ended up losing over $55 million dollars. This very expensive lesson occurred because the company tried to save a few dollars and minimize its costs by not sending a specialist to Sicily to check on the trees prior to purchase.

Inappropriate production sites have also left deep wounds in many other firms. One U.S. food processor built a pineapple cannery at the delta of a river in Mexico. Since the pineapple plantation was located upstream, the company planned to float the ripe fruit down to the cannery on barges. To its dismay, however, the firm soon discovered that at harvest time the river current was far too strong for barge traffic. Since no other feasible alternative method of transportation existed, the plant was closed. The new equipment was sold for a fraction of its original cost to a Mexican group that immediately relocated the cannery. This seemingly simple navigational oversight proved quite expensive to the firm.

The Hanna Mining Company experienced similar logistical problems in Brazil. One of the basic strategies of the firm involved its ability to supply extract ore at increasing rates over time. Since a small-scale operation could not prove profitable, the company decided that by expanding every year it would become a profitable operation by the time the firm was able to export two million tons of ore. Few initial problems developed. The company, however, was unable to expand its operations as expected because local transportation facilities were inadequate. In this case, the firm's strategy failed because it had no way to transport the ore to market even though it maintained the capability to extract the required ore. (It should be noted that Hanna Mining reports that this was not a foreseeable problem since the local railroad authorities failed to fulfill the contract's maximum delivery requirement.)

In another example, a French firm set up a timber mill in East Africa and was all set to open the mill when the French realized that usually there was not enough electrical power in the area to run the mill. Unfortunately, there may never be. The firm had to dismantle this useless mill.

Sometimes it is not the plant location that is the problem, but the plant layout. For example, an English pulp and paper company entered into a joint venture arrangement with another British firm hoping to utilize the timber resources of British Columbia. They obtained a concession of enormous timberland acreage. The sawmill, however, was designed and set up by British engineers who were unfamiliar with the characteristics of British Columbian lumber. As a result, the mill was constructed with a setup that was not flexible enough to adjust to the numerous varieties and sizes of Canadian trees. Within three years the firms sold the mill at a substantial loss.

In another misunderstanding, a British firm returned a large shipment of American-made textile machinery motors, believing it had not received the motors it thought that it had ordered. Apparently, a right-handed motor in an English mill is considered a left-handed motor in the United States. Americans look at the production run from downstream and thus see the motor in an opposite manner than do the British who view things from the start of the production run.

PRODUCT

In developed countries, we often take for granted the vast array of products available for sale. In many countries, however, such product variety and selection does not exist. The assumption that the absence of a product from an economy automatically indicates a potentially good or profitable market has led a number of companies down a thorny path. More than one company has failed to consider that even if the local consumers can afford the product, they may not really want it or may be interested in it only if it is substantially modified to fit their local tastes and preferences.

These modifications, known as adaptations, exist in two major forms: product and package. Product modification, or the alteration of the physical product, is occasionally required for the product to conform to local tastes or local conditions. Adaptation of the package is often necessary to attract the customer to the product or to maintain the product's integrity in a unique environment. Occasionally, a firm is forced to modify both the package and the product to create a suitable product for the new market.

Product Adaptation

Apple Computer entered the Japanese market before IBM, but it failed to take advantage of its head start. Apple tried to sell its U.S. models in Japan without modifying them. No efforts were made to even translate the user's manual into Japanese. Only after IBM entered the market using a customized approach did Apple realize its mistakes. Now that the company has translated its manual and has made some other changes, it is doing much better.

Similarly, Proctor and Gamble encountered problems with the Japanese diaper market. After years of research, the company uncovered the problem: Japanese parents change diapers far more frequently than Americans do but usually do not have the storage space of American homes. Thus, larger boxes of disposable diapers posed a storage problem for the average Japanese family. Once Proctor and Gamble began producing thinner diapers sold in a smaller box, the popularity of the new diapers, Ultra Pampers, spread like a baby's rash and now it is the leading brand in Japan.

The Campbell Soup Company discovered that product modification can be an easier road to travel than consumer education when it tried to market its condensed soups in Great Britain. The company had used market-testing methods to confirm a British interest in its soups and had also priced the soup competitively. But initial sales were low, a result of the failure of the British to understand that Campbell's Soup was indeed priced competitively. The British were accustomed to buying canned soup but not in the condensed form. Therefore, it appeared to them that they were buying half as much soup for the same amount of money. The Campbell Soup Company was faced with two choices: It could try to hurriedly masseducate the British buying public or it could alter the product. It wisely chose to modify its product by adding water so that its soups would be like the soups already produced and found on the grocery shelves.

General Foods experienced similar difficulties when it tried to sell its American-style Jell-O in Great Britain. Although the package of Jell-O contained the normal powdered substance Americans expect when buying Jell-O, the British simply were not interested. In Great Britain, the product is generally sold in its jelled form. To a Briton, if it does not jiggle and look ready to eat, then it simply isn't "proper." By quickly changing its product to conform to the British norm, General Foods averted a possible disaster.

The sale of cigarettes outside the home country has been equally exasperating for several companies. The common presumption that all peoples enjoy identical products has often proven erroneous; in fact, some form of product modification is usually necessary to gain market success. The failure to make the needed alteration, even though possibly a slight one, can radically hurt sales. More than one firm, for example, has encountered difficulties trying to sell filter-tipped cigarettes in the less developed countries. Consumers of wealthier nations, more aware of the health risks of smoking, are quite willing to pay a bit more for filtered cigarettes. In poor countries where life expectancy is often less than 30 years, the threat of death from lung cancer is lessened. Even if aware of the risks, the local smoker can usually neither afford the extra cost of the filtered cigarettes nor become too concerned about developing lung cancer at an advanced age. Consequently, the market for filtered cigarettes in these countries is typically sluggish. Often the only modification needed to increase sales is the removal of the filter and the accompanying reduction in price.

Some products may require more technical modification, however. Obviously, if the electrical current available in a potential market is different from the home country market, then electrical products require adaptation before introduction. Measurement systems vary between countries, and often components need to be modified to adhere to local standards. Product sizes must also be considered. A British firm, for example, experienced problems selling in Japan until it remodeled its product one-sixteenth of an inch to conform to Japanese specifications. Such small differences can easily cause major headaches for manufacturers. Fortunately, most companies quickly learn of these local standards and conditions and seldom introduce a totally inappropriate product. A much more difficult task is the detection of the subtle technical differences and the needed modifications.

In one such case, Star Manufacturing Co., Ltd of Japan quickly realized that it had introduced a computer printer that didn't arouse American interest. The printer that had sold well in Japan did poorly in the United States because Americans wanted better graphics. The printer was soon modified and sales picked up immediately.

In another case, a duplicating machine manufacturer ran into serious problems in one country when it assumed that the quality paper required for use in its machines would be available. The local government owned its own paper company and unfortunately, the paper size and quality were not highly standardized. Thus, the imported machines could not accommodate the varying characteristics. Due to the government's pride in its paper facilities, however, importation of the paper required was not allowed. The machines sat idle, and the company's market was quickly closed. The company should have learned of this problem prior to its market entry.

It could then have requested permission to import the correct paper, or it could have modified its machines to accommodate the local paper. Had neither been possible, the firm would have known *not* to market its products in that country.

Similarly, Polaroid planned to introduce a slide copier as a central piece of its 1989 product line for both U.S. and European markets. Unfortunately, the engineers failed to realize that standard paper sizes vary. Therefore, the copier would not work using standard European paper. Hasty modifications were made, but not without extra costs.

Marketing its liquid detergents in Europe proved to be an equal challenge for Proctor and Gamble since European washing machines dispense powdered detergents. Adapters to the machines were not a feasible option because each brand of machine required a different design. Proctor and Gamble eventually came up with the solution: A plastic ball was supplied with each bottle of detergent. The "dosing ball" could be filled with detergent and placed in each load of laundry. Proctor and Gamble now holds 50 percent of the liquid detergent market in Europe.

Refrigerator manufacturers from Western nations initially encountered great difficulty in selling their products in Japan. The refrigerator motors were the major problem; they were simply too noisy for the typical Japanese home that was often built with literally paper thin walls. Sears is cited as one of the companies most successful in the sale of Western refrigerators in Japan. It achieved this status by designing a refrigerator specifically for use under the local conditions.

General Motors of Canada likewise experienced major technical problems with one of its cars in Iraq. It shipped 13,500 Chevrolet Malibu automobiles there only to discover that the cars were mechanically unfit for the hot and dusty climate. Iraq refused delivery of the remaining 12,000 autos that had been ordered until GM modified the vehicles so that they performed more reliably. GM tripled its number of engineers and mechanics in Baghdad, but by the time the company figured out that supplementary air filters and different clutches would eliminate the mechanical failures, it began to encounter political problems. Thus, 12,000 automobiles specially designed for desert driving collected snow in Canada while GM waited for the political dust to settle.

An American tire producer also had to make unexpected major adjustments after opening a plant in France. Based on its previous success in France, the tire manufacturer built a new production facility without conducting any market research. Due to the changing driving habits of the French, however, new kinds of tires were required and the manufacturer was forced to make adjustments. The company learned its lesson, of course. It hired a market research executive before building its next plant.

The necessity for product adaptation has existed for hundreds of years. England's East India Company possibly lost control of India in 1857 because it failed to modify a product it provided. In those days bullets were often encased in pig wax, and the tops had to be bitten off before the bullets could be fired. The Asian Indian soldiers were furious when they discovered the pig wax since it was against their religion to eat pork. The soldiers revolted and hundreds were killed on both sides before peace was restored. The bullets were modified, but the East India Company lost control of India to the British Crown.[3]

Improper product modification can also lead to misery. China discovered this when it shipped shoes to Egypt. It had tried to make the shoes more appealing to the Egyptians by placing Arabic characters on the soles of the shoes. Unfortunately, the designers did not know Arabic and merely copied words from other material. The words they chose meant "God." It required China's ambassador to Egypt to alleviate the tension that resulted from this mistake.

Sometimes the modified product inadvertently reaches the wrong market. This too can cause problems. Not long ago, for example, one company received a great deal of unwanted attention from U.S. parents who purchased a talking doll they believed said, "Kill Mommy." These dolls, made in Hong Kong but shipped from Japan to many parts of the world, carried messages in the language of the country of destination. A packing error, however, caused some Spanish-speaking dolls to be sent to the United States. The Spanish message was "Quiero Mommy," which means "I love Mommy," but the poor quality sound reproduction and the language difference altered the message and caused a media sensation.

Taste/Style

One variable often requiring modification is taste. Both the food and tobacco industries can attest to this. Philip Morris, Inc. encountered well-publicized problems when it tried to sell its U.S. blends in Canada. Many other companies have experienced similar difficulties in other countries. Most cigarette firms believe that "it is better to switch than fight," and cigarettes are now generally blended in deference to local taste preferences.

Vast numbers of food products have required taste adaptations in order to appeal to local consumers. General Foods experienced some problems and had to alter some of its coffees and foods to attract European and Japanese palates. The Campbell Soup Company also was forced to change the flavor of some of its soups (notably the tomato soup) to suit European preferences. Many soft drinks have been modified to gain market acceptance in various parts of the world. Often all that is necessary is a subtle change, but without such variation, sales may slump. Both General Foods and the Campbell Soup Company have enjoyed overseas success because they realized this and acted accordingly. Nestle's has also successfully introduced dozens of blends of its Nescafé instant coffee around the world.

Fast food chains have been especially quick to modify their offerings. McDonald's, for example, adjusts its menu for each foreign market. It has sold beer in Germany, wine in France, mutton pot pies in Australia, and McSpaghetti in the Philippines. Burger King in Venezuela does not use sesame seed buns, the milkshakes there are sweeter and creamier, and even the ketchup is much sweeter. Wendy's serves shrimp cake sandwiches in Japan. Shaky's sells chorizo in Mexico and squid in Japan. Arby's dropped its ham sandwiches from its menus in the Middle East. Kentucky Fried Chicken (KFC) serves "chips" rather than "fries" in England, and has added rice and smoked chicken to its menus in Japan. KFC also initiated one of the more unique product modifications; in order to sell its chicken in Israel, it introduced kosher chicken.

An exception to this successful taste modification has been Pop-Tarts. The toaster pastries, which have proved to be quite a successful product in the United States, were unpopular in Britain. Not only was the taste considered too sweet there, but most potential buyers at the time did not own toasters that could correctly warm the product. But U.S. companies are not only ones that have found local tastes different from those at home. European soups, for example, are considered too salty by most Americans and have not sold well on U.S. grocery shelves.

Food and tobacco manufacturers have not borne the effects of consumer preference alone. Style is another important ingredient in the product mix, and failure to reflect local style choices is also likely to cause financial losses for a company. Ford experienced well-publicized problems in Europe during the 1960s, partly as a result of the amount of "Americanization" being introduced to the look of its European cars. Earlier style lines of Ford's European cars sold well in Europe because of their simple sleekness, which was favored by the local people. When the more traditional aspects of the American automobile (i.e., wideness, heaviness, length) were incorporated into models of the 1960s, sales slumped. The sales resistance came to a halt when the cars produced once again reflected European tastes.

The clothing manufacturer Cluett, Peabody may have had similar problems because its Belgian factory was closed after only three years. Cluett blames high costs for the closing, but Belgian retailers claim it was really due to a complaisant Belgian management that assented to American styling, pricing, and sizing that were not in harmony with European tastes and budgets. Either cause for failure could have been eliminated through appropriate preliminary research and implementation of the indicated modifications.

PACKAGE

In many markets, the product may be quite acceptable but still not sell well if inappropriately packaged. Packages play two key roles in marketing – they promote the product and they protect it. Packages that require long-distance shipping must be capable of withstanding the journey. Many companies have endeavored to export their products only to witness the return of crushed and partially empty containers. Others have tried to ship perishable goods by means requiring months for delivery. Still others have placed the goods in packages unable to withstand moisture (or other unique conditions).

In one such case, a firm in Taiwan shipped some drinking glasses to the Middle East. The company used wooden crates and padded the glasses with hay. Most of the glasses, however, were broken by the time they reached their destination. As the crates traveled into the drier Middle East, the moisture content of the hay dropped. By the time the crates were delivered, the thin straw offered almost no protection. What works well in one part of the world doesn't necessarily work well everywhere.

A similar problem was encountered by another Taiwanese firm. The Iranians refused payment on a shipment of wool because they claimed that the shipper lied about the weight of the shipment. After expensive delays, it was discovered that wool originating in humid countries (such as Taiwan) loses moisture when shipped to dry countries (like Iran), and therefore weighs less after being shipped.

In some climates, packages must be specially designed to assure product survival. Quaker Oats, for example, uses special vacuum-sealed tins to protect its products that are sold in hot and humid countries.

Local storage conditions also vary, and the package must be an appropriate size and shape. Coca-Cola tried to introduce the two-liter plastic bottle in Spain, but market entry was difficult. The company soon discovered that few Spaniards had refrigerator doors with compartments large enough to accommodate the large-size bottle.

Detergents must also be packaged differently to sell well in various countries. Americans, for example, are less concerned than Germans with such details as chemical actions and how the detergent actually works. The German package, therefore, must be modified to contain this extra information considered important by the consumer in that country.

Seemingly harmless package labels have sometimes proved to be embarrassing to the company or even insulting to its potential consumers. One soft drink company inadvertently offended some of its customers in the Arab world because its labels incorporated six pointed stars. The stars were only considered to be a decoration by the firm, but they were interpreted by the Arabs as reflecting pro-Israeli sentiments. Naturally, the label had to be altered. Another company printed the label on its product in ten languages, including Hebrew, and then tried to market it in Arab countries.

Although many people do not realize it, the swastika was not created by Nazi Germany as the party emblem and symbol of anti-Semitism. In fact, it has been used for centuries as a symbol of good luck in many countries. In India, M. P. Been Products, Ltd has been using the symbol on many of its packages as a sort of company logo. However, when its managers decided to launch a new beer described as "German Pilsner," the combination of the beer name and the swastika on the same label was not well received.

Likewise, medical containers made in the United States drew a great deal of unwanted attention when they were used in Great Britain. The containers carried the instructions "Take off top and push in bottom." This message, considered harmless in the United Sates, bore very sexual and humorous connotations for the British. Needless to say, the containers were soon modified.

In areas where many of the people are illiterate, the label usually depicts a picture of what the package contains. This very logical practice proved to be quite perplexing to one big company. It tried to sell baby food in an African nation by using its regular label, which showed a baby and stated the type of baby food in the jar. Unfortunately, the local population took one look at the labels and interpreted them to mean that the jars contained ground-up babies. Sales, of course, were terrible.

Some European dry soup producers have solved their marketing problems in the United States by altering their labels. Rather than trying to change the product, they merely developed different uses for the product and stated this on the package label. European dried soups are packaged identically but labeled differently when sold in America. The U.S. package emphasizes the use of the product as a sauce or dip. As expected, U.S. sales were much better once the firm stressed the nonsoup use.

Even something as innocuous as a wrapping can cause trouble. A New York exporter agreed to send some products to an Arab country and thoughtlessly wrapped the goods in local newspapers for shipment. The customer was arrested and his goods confiscated when the Arab customs inspectors opened up the packages and found that the wrappings used were Jewish newspapers.

Another American firm also blundered in the Middle East. A carefully detailed business proposal that had required a great deal of preparation was sent to Saudi Arabia. The proposal, an excellent one, was bound with a pigskin cover and so was never even read. (Recall that Muslims are required to avoid pig products.)

The use of numbers provides another source of blunders. Each country has its own special lucky and unlucky numbers, and using the wrong number can indeed be unlucky. A U.S. golf ball manufacturer, for example, tried to sell golf balls packaged in groups of four to the Japanese. Problems arose because the pronunciation of the word "four" in Japanese also sounds like the Japanese word for "death." The number four, therefore, is considered undesirable, and items grouped into fours simply don't sell well.

U.S. airlines with routes between Japan and Hawaii initially experienced very erratic success. Some days the flights were fully booked, while other days the planes flew nearly empty. It took some time, but the airlines eventually figured out the problem. Apparently, the Japanese have traditional days that are considered good for weddings. These "lucky days" are naturally followed by honeymoons, and Hawaii is a favored destination. In order to even out the flying load, the airlines began offering discounts for the days when the honeymooners were not flying.

Color

The choice of package and product coloring can be tricky. Sometimes companies have failed to sell their products overseas and have never known why. Often the reason was a simple one: the product or its container was merely an inappropriate color.

Green, for instance, is often associated with disease in countries that have dense, green jungles but is associated with cosmetics by the French, Dutch, and Swedes. Various colors represent death. Black signifies death to Americans and many Europeans, while in Japan and many other Asian countries white represents death. Latin Americans generally associate purple with death, but dark red is the appropriate mourning color along the Ivory Coast. And even though white is the color representing death to some, it expresses joy to those living in Ghana. In many countries, bright colors such as yellow and orange express joy. To most of the world, blue is thought to be a masculine color, but it is not as manly as red in the United Kingdom or France. In Iran, however, blue represents an undesirable color. Although Americans believe pink to be the foremost feminine color, most of the rest of the world considers yellow to be the most feminine color. Considered blasphemous in some African countries, red is generally regarded as a color reflecting wealth or luxury elsewhere. A red circle has been successfully used on many packages sold in Latin America, but it is unpopular in some parts of Asia where it conjures up images of the Japanese flag.

Pictures of flowers can be found on many package labels, but there too caution is required. Certain flowers and their colors can convey hidden messages. In France and many countries that have experienced a British influence, the white lily is often used for funerals. Mexicans, though, use lilies to lift superstitious spells. A purple flower symbolizes death to a Brazilian, while yellow flowers represent death or disrespect in Mexico. In France and the Soviet Union, however, the yellow flower signifies infidelity.

For instance, United Airlines had start-up problems with its initial flights from Hong Kong. It seems that the company handed out white carnations without realizing that, to many Asians, such flowers represent death and bad luck. Thus, they soon switched to red carnations.

SUMMARY

Product and package modifications are often required to enhance a product's appeal to the foreign consumer. Sometimes the alterations are minor; other times they are more complex. Market testing can help a firm avoid the entry of an inappropriate product; the failure to initiate such studies or develop thorough ones has led a number of companies to blunder.

In all fairness to multinational firms, however, market tests can be quite tricky to initiate and conduct. It is difficult indeed to cover all the bases, and one of the hardest tasks is the identification of the proper testing locations. Since firms cannot always afford to test each product everywhere, sample areas are normally identified as being representative of a country or region. Some companies have used an area of France for their West European test market. Others have used Belgium. Each firm must determine the region most appropriate for its product. This is no easy task. In fact, a combination of locations may be necessary. Wherever these places are, though, they must be found, because market testing is essential to product success.

3
NAMES

Shakespeare once queried, "What's in a name?" A number of business people, after a bit of international marketing, might appropriately respond, "More than you might think." Many companies have discovered that even something as seemingly innocuous as a name can prove to be insulting and embarrassing to certain consumers. Both product and company names can fall prey to such troubles.

PRODUCT NAMES

Product names often take on various unintended and hidden meanings. The experience of a major soapmaker serves as a classic example. When this company was considering a name for a new soap powder it wished to market internationally, it wisely ran a translation test of the proposed soap name in 50 major languages. In English and most of the major European languages, the name meant "dainty." In other tongues, however, the soap name did not translate so appropriately. In Gaelic it became "song," in Flemish it meant "aloof," and in the language of one African tribe it said "horse." In Persia, the name was translated as "hazy" or "dim-witted," and to the Koreans, the name sounded like a person out of his mind. Finally, in all of the Slavic languages, the name was considered obscene and offensive. Naturally, the proposed name was hastily abandoned. This experience, though, demonstrates the importance of a name and how carefully it should be considered prior to the introduction of a product.

Unusual Problems

"Golden Harp Superior Pilsner" is hard enough to say in English, but it is even more difficult to say if English is not your mother tongue. In Malaysia (where they do not even have harps), the words are very difficult to pronounce and certainly do not sound like the name of a beer. Therefore, Ogilvy and Mather shortened the product's name to Goldie and used a sexy blonde to promote the brew. The problem was that the label still read "Golden Harp Superior Pilsner," so when Malaysians ordered a "Goldie" all they usually got from the bartender was a blank stare. The product was eventually withdrawn.

Today, more and more firms are initiating research in hopes of avoiding costly and embarrassing mistakes. Even the largest and most sophisticated firms are not immune to the difficulties of product-name interpretation. For example, when the Coca-Cola Company was planning its strategy for marketing in China in the 1920s, it wanted to introduce its product with the English pronunciation of "Coca-Cola." A translator developed a group of Chinese characters that, when pronounced, sounded like the product name. These characters were placed on the cola bottles and marketed. Was it any wonder that sales levels were low? The characters actually translated to mean "a wax-flattened mare" or "bite the wax tadpole." Since the product was new, sound was unimportant to the consumers; meaning was vital. Today Coca-Cola is again marketing its cola in China. The new characters used on the bottle translate to "happiness in the mouth." From its first marketing attempts, Coca-Cola learned a valuable lesson in international marketing.

Olympia reportedly tried to introduce a photo copier in Chile under the name ROTO. The copiers, however, did not sell well. Why? Two possible explanations: (1) *roto* is the Spanish word for "broken," and (2) *roto* is the word used to delineate the lowest class in Chile.

General Motors was faced with a somewhat similar problem. It was troubled by the lack of enthusiasm among the Puerto Rican auto dealers for its recently introduced Chevrolet Nova. The word *nova* means "star" when translated literally. However, when spoken, it sounds like "no va," which in Spanish means "it does not go." This obviously did little to increase consumer confidence in the new vehicle. To remedy the situation, General Motors changed the automobile name to Caribe and sales increased.

Other car manufacturers have experienced comparable situations. In fact, problems often develop with the names used in international automobile promotions. For example, difficulties arose during the translation of the name of an American car, the Randan. Apparently this name was interpreted by some Japanese to mean "idiot." Likewise, an American Motors Corporation car, the Matador, usually conjures up images of virility and strength, but in Puerto Rico the name means "killer" – not a favorable connotation in a place with high traffic fatality rates.

Apache pickup trucks do not sell well to most American Indians – that is, except to Apaches. This type of problem is not unique to Chevrolet nor is it new. Studebaker introduced the Dictator back in 1927 but had to discontinue the line in 1936 when politics in Italy and Germany drew worldwide attention.

Initial sales of Nissan's sports car, the Fair Lady, were so disappointing in the United States that management decided to investigate the cause. The conclusion: the name *fair lady* was not sporty enough. Thus, the name was changed to 240 Z and the car became one of the most successful Nissan has ever launched.

Ford encountered problems with some of its cars as well. It introduced a low-cost truck, the Fiera, into some of the less-developed countries. Unfortunately the name meant "ugly old woman" in Spanish. Needless to say, this name did not encourage sales. Ford also experienced slow sales when it introduced a top-of-the-line automobile, the Comet, in Mexico under the name Caliente. The puzzlingly low sales levels were finally understood when Ford discovered that *caliente* is slang for "streetwalker." Additional headaches were reportedly experienced when Ford's Pinto was briefly introduced in Brazil under its English name. The name was speedily changed to Corcel (which means "horse" in Portuguese) after Ford discovered that the Portuguese slang translation of *pinto* is a "small male appendage."

The naming of a new automobile model to be marketed in Germany by Rolls Royce was a difficult undertaking. The company felt that the English name, Silver Mist, was very appealing but discovered that the name would undoubtedly not capture the German market as hoped. In German, the translated meaning of *mist* is actually "excrement," and the Germans could not possibly have found such a name attractive. Unfortunately, the Sunbeam Corporation did not learn of this particular translation problem in time and attempted to enter the German market advertising its new mist-producing hair curling iron as the Mist-Stick. As should have been expected, the Germans had no interest in a "dung" or "manure" wand.

In the early 1980s, a German beer company launched a new brand in West Africa and named it EKU. Sales were uneven, and it took the firm two years to figure out the cause. Foreigners and some local tribe members purchased the beer, but one important tribe totally avoided it. Apparently *EKU* was the local slang word in that tribe for "excrement." As word spread, members of other tribes and even the foreigners started drinking it less. In the meantime, however, more than a few natives enjoyed watching outsiders consume EKU. The name was eventually dropped.

Firms occasionally try to enter the foreign market promoting a product bearing an untranslated name. Sometimes this tactic works, but other times it does not work as well as expected. At least one global firm can attest to this. The company consistently marketed one of its pieces of equipment under the name Grab Bucket. To its chagrin, the firm learned that in Germany it was actually advertising the sale of cemetery plot flowers. In German, the word *grab* is interpreted as "grave," and the word *bucket* is pronounced like "bouquet." So because of these linguistic anomalies, the company did not appear to be selling what it thought it was.

Many companies have suffered similar pitfalls. A U.S. company was taken by surprise when it introduced its product in Latin America and learned that the name of the product meant "jackass oil" in Spanish. Another well-intentioned firm sold shampoo in Brazil under the name Evitol. Little did it realize that it was claiming to be selling a "dandruff contraceptive." A manufacturing company sold its machines in the Soviet Union under the name Bardak, a word that signifies a brothel in Russian. One American product failed to capture the Swedish market when the product name was translated to "enema," which the product was not. Kellogg has done fairly well with its sales of cereals overseas, but even it had to rename its Bran Buds cereal in Sweden when the company discovered that the name translates roughly to "burned farmer." Parker Pen sells a ballpen, or ball-point, in most countries under the name Jotter. However, it wisely uses other names in some Latin American markets because *jotter* sometimes means "jockstrap."

Product names can take on equally unanticipated meanings when marketed by foreign companies in the United States. For instance, a Finnish brewery introduced two new beverages in the United States – Koff beer and Siff beer. Is it any wonder that sales were sluggish? Another name, unappealing to Americans, can be found on the package of a delicious chocolate and fruit product sold in the European deli. The chocolate concoction has the undesirable English name, Zit. Likewise, Sic (a French soft drink), Super Piss (a Finnish product for unfreezing car doors), and Bum (a Spanish potato chip) will probably not be sold in the United States.

An Australian brewer sells a popular beer in Australia by the name of XXXX which is pronounced "four X's." The company planned to export this beer to the United States until it learned that the Americans were already familiar with Fourex – a brand of condoms.

The reported troubles of an American company that markets Pet milk serves as another example. This firm supposedly experienced difficulties introducing its product in French-speaking areas. It seems that the word *pet* in French means, among other things, "to break wind." And had Colgate-Palmolive attempted to gain market entry with its Cue toothpaste in French-speaking regions, it too would have encountered comparable problems. *Cue* is a pornographic word in French.

An American woman will long remember her international experience with Coca-Cola. She was dispensing sample tasters of Fresca soda pop when she unintentionally elicited a great deal of laughter from passersby. She only later realized the cause when she discovered that in Mexican slang the word *fresca* means "lesbian."

Close examination of foreign markets and language differences are necessary and should be required before a product's domestically successful name is introduced abroad. Unfortunately, this simple warning is sometimes neglected in a company's enthusiasm to plunge into overseas marketing operations. Manufacturers often assume that products that have enjoyed domestic success will naturally receive the same reception overseas. However, this is not always the case as the following examples demonstrate. Princess Housewares, Inc., a large U.S. appliance manufacturer, introduced a line of electric housewares in the German market. The company's brand name, well known and highly regarded in the United States, was relatively unknown in Germany. Its name, though, which had a definite American sound, turned out to be a real drawback to sales since the German consumers disliked the American association. Similarly, in the early 1960s General Mills spent over $1.4 million advertising its Betty Crocker cake mixes in an effort to gain entry into the British market. The costly promotion, though, did not achieve the expected positive results. Although research revealed that the product itself was quite acceptable, the British reportedly could not identify with the exotic names given to the cake mixes.

Name adaptations sometimes prove to be winners; other times they do not. The Johnson Wax Company successfully introduced its product Pledge in Germany under the name Pronto, but problems arose when the product entered the market in the Netherlands as Pliz. In Dutch, the pronunciation of Pliz sounds like "piss." Understandably, it was rather difficult for the customer of the conventional Dutch grocery store to ask for the product.

Sometimes the required change in the product name is a rather simple one. Wrigley, for example, merely altered the spelling of its Spearmint chewing gum to Speermint to aid in the German pronunciation of the flavor. Maxwell House proved slightly more difficult. The name was changed to Maxwell Kaffee in Germany, Legal in France, and Monky in Spain.

As evidenced, firms have blundered by changing product names and by failing to alter names. This is not to say, however, that one is "damned if you do and damned if you don't." Adequate name assessments prior to market introduction can reduce potential name blunders.

Obscene Meanings

Inappropriate product names sometimes prove to be quite humorous, but in a number of cases the names have actually borne fairly obscene implications and connotations. A few illustrations of this type of blunder follow.

Birds Eye considered itself quite fortunate when it discovered that a proposed name for one of its fish food products was inappropriate. Wisely, the company decided against the name when it uncovered that the name translated to "genitals."

Not all firms have been so lucky, however. A well-known oil company was caught in an embarrassing situation when it learned of the inadvertently indecent name it had chosen for its products. The company established operations in Indonesia and manufactured machinery displaying the name Nonox. One can imagine the firm's discomfort when it was informed that "Nonox" sounded similar to the Javanese slang word *nonok* — a word comparable to the American idiom for female "private parts."

Obviously the employees who proposed the name Joni for a new facial cream that was to be marketed in India had never read the erotic Indian classic *Kama Sutra*. If they had, they would surely have known that the Hindu word *joni* represents the most intimate areas of the female body.

The example of a vitamin product introduced in South America serves as a final illustration of how product names can unintentionally become obscenities. In this case, a company introduced its vitamins as Fundavit and boasted that they satisfied the fundamental vitamin requirements. The name had to be modified when the firm learned that *fundola* in Spanish stands for the backside of an attractive young woman.

Other Offensive Names

As illustrated, certain product name choices can create embarrassing situations for companies when the names are interpreted as indecencies. On occasion, a company chooses a name that, although not obscene, turns out to be in poor taste and offensive to certain groups of people. One example is the name Black Nikka, chosen for a brand of Japanese whiskey sold in the United States and found to be demeaning by some black Americans. Consider also the bold experiment in international marketing that brought together the state-controlled tobacco monopolies of five countries (France, Italy, Portugal, Austria, and Japan) to launch a major promotion of a new brand of cigarettes, Champagne. This venture proved to be an embarrassment to the French government, and the case wound up in the international law courts with the French champagne producers in a fury. These producers claimed that the use of the word *champagne* as a brand name "is deplorable, and the connection with health hazards may permanently damage our image."[4]

Yves St. Laurent drew some unwanted criticism when it named a new fragrance Opium. Even though the advertising campaign was voted the best of 1978 by the Fragrance Foundation, it created a storm of protest. Some people viewed it as poor judgment to name a fragrance after an illegal drug. The original French slogan "Pour celles qui s'adonnet à Yves St. Laurent" (For those who are addicted to Yves St. Laurent) only tended to reinforce the problematic connotations of the fragrance's name. The Chinese also considered the use of the name Opium to be a racial slur. Public pressure eventually forced the company to discontinue the sales promotion in some places.

COMPANY NAMES

Product names are not the only names that can generate company blunders. If a firm name is misinterpreted or incorrectly translated, it too can cause humorous, obscene, offensive, or unexpected situations. A number of examples are described in the following paragraphs.

Colonel Sanders (KFC) experienced resistance while marketing its chicken in Germany because some folks connected the word *colonel* with the U.S. military, which is not popular with all Germans. And because Brazilians have trouble pronouncing "Kentucky Fried Chicken," the name Sanders was used there.

A private Egyptian airline, Misair, proved to be rather unpopular with the French nationals. Could the fact that the name, when pronounced, meant "misery" in French have contributed to the airline's plight? Another airline trying to gain acceptance in Australia only complicated matters when it chose the firm name EMU. The emu is an Australian bird that is incapable of flying. But EMU was not the only company to run into snags while conducting business in Australia. The AMF Corporation was forced to change its name. Why? Because AMF is the official designation for the Australian Military Forces. Similarly, Sears was forbidden to use its unchanged name in Spain. The company commanded respect and enjoyed a good reputation there; but since the Castilian Spanish pronunciation of Sears sounded much like "Seat" (the name of Spain's largest car manufacturer), Seat forced Sears to incorporate the name Roebuck on all its products.

When Esso realized that its name phonetically meant "stalled car," it understood why it had had difficulties in the Japanese market. And was it any wonder that Ford ran into unexpected low sales levels in Spain? Apparently its cars were not popular with certain groups; some of the locals were interpreting the name Ford to mean "*F*abrica *O*rdinaria *R*eparaciones *D*iariamente" (Ordinarily, make repairs daily). The Vicks Company, however, was more fortunate. It discovered that in German "Vicks" sounds like the most crude slang equivalent of intercourse and was able to change its name to an acceptable Wicks.

As a final illustration, consider the trade magazine that promoted giftware and launched a worldwide circulation effort. The magazine used the word *gift* in its title and as part of its name. When it was later revealed that gift is the German word for "poison," a red-faced publishing executive supposedly retorted that the Germans should simply find a new word for poison.

Of course, not all companies have been forced to change their names. In fact, some of them have traveled quite well. Kodak may be the most famous example. A research team deliberately "developed" this name after carefully searching for a word that was pronounceable everywhere but had no specific meaning anywhere. Exxon is another such name that was reportedly accepted only after a lengthy and expensive computer-assisted search.

SUMMARY

Multinational corporations have experienced many unexpected troubles concerning company or product names, and even attempts to alter names have led to blunders. It should be evident that careful planning and study of the potential market are necessary as name adaptation can be every bit as important as product or package modification.

4
MARKETING

The field of marketing has probably experienced the most corporate headaches. The old adage "If something can go wrong, it will" seems especially true for marketing managers; they have undoubtedly blundered every single marketing task imaginable.

Early blunders often occurred because people forgot that cultures vary from country to country. Unfortunately, this error continues to be made. A print advertisement for a men's cologne, for example, recently pictured a man and his dog in an American rural setting. The picture was well accepted in America but was not effective when used in northern Africa. The advertiser simply assumed that the American "man's best friend" was loved everywhere when, in fact, Muslims usually consider dogs to be either signs of bad luck or symbols of uncleanliness. Neither interpretation helped sales of the cologne.

Proctor and Gamble blundered in Japan when trying to sell Camay soap. It seems that the company aired a popular European television advertisement that showed a woman bathing. In the ad, her husband enters the bathroom and touches her approvingly. The Japanese, however, considered this behavior to be inappropriate and in poor taste for television. Such ads are no longer used in Japan, and as a result Proctor and Gamble is now doing much better there.

A well-known American designer tried to launch a new fragrance in Latin America. The advertising message emphasized the perfume's fresh camellia scent. Naturally, sales were slow there because camellias are flowers used for funerals in most of Latin America.

Proctor and Gamble's original Japanese promotion of Cheer laundry detergent boasted that the detergent was effective at "all water temperatures." The slogan proved successful in America because Americans wash their laundry in many different temperatures depending on the preference of the consumer. However, the Japanese wash most clothes in cold water so the promotion was almost meaningless to them. Proctor and Gamble changed its approach and ran ads touting Cheer's superior cleaning in cold water. Now Cheer sells much better in Japan.

Not all blunders, of course, are due to the erroneous assumption that what works at home will always work abroad also. Sometimes, the promotional campaign is just launched at the wrong time. Timing is one of the most critical elements in the launching of a new product. Most firms understand this and also recognize that various cultures perceive time differently. Since some nationalities are more conscious of time factors than others, companies must often allocate extra time and give extra care to assure that its marketing campaign is completed as scheduled. One firm aware of these constraints properly timed everything, or so it thought. Various types of promotional activities were arranged for its product's market entries, but one thing was overlooked – the product. Because someone forgot to assure its availability, all of the expensive, well-planned promotions became meaningless.

Or take the Israel Government Tourist Office's decision to wisely suspend an ad campaign in the Netherlands proclaiming that Tel Aviv and Jerusalem were only "a stone's throw" apart. The timing of the ad was unfortunate as real stone throwing was actually occurring in the country at the time.

PROMOTIONS

Promotional efforts often misfire; some downfalls, though, are more predictable than others. A cosmetics firm attempted to sell its lipstick in Japan using a television ad that depicted Nero coming to life just as a pretty woman wearing the lipstick strolled by. This hard sell was resented by the Japanese women who had no real idea of who Nero was. If a firm decides to use historical figures in promotional campaigns, it is well advised to first consider using locally known historical figures.

In a different type of case, a company formed a joint venture with an Asian firm. Both companies believed everything to be in order. Their plan included a large production run and a simultaneous, large promotional effort. The production process ran smoothly, but the expected promotional efforts never materialized. Each company had assumed that the other would coordinate and pay for all promotional activities. In fact, each firm simply assumed the customs of its own country's business practices and was not prepared to accept the country's norm of the other firm. Neither company would have agreed to the venture had it thought that it would be responsible for promotion costs. The promotion was never undertaken, and the joint venture eventually broke up.

One of United Airlines' promotional campaigns used the slogan "We know the Orient." In the ads, the names of Far Eastern countries were printed below the pictures of foreign coins. Sadly, the slogan was not very convincing because the coins and countries did not match up.

Another American corporation believed it had developed a good promotional plan when it decided to distribute simulated old coins displaying the company logo. To make the coins appear a bit more realistic, the company placed a monetary value on them and, to avoid any chance of claims of counterfeiting, it used the obviously phony value of $1 billion. The coins were passed out at a trade show in West Germany but, to the company's surprise, the coins seemed to anger the locals. Apparently the Germans felt that the company was trying to show off American wealth, and they resented this impression. The coins would have been more effective if they had displayed some denomination of the German mark.

In addition to being aware of cultural content in promotion, more and more firms are realizing they must scrutinize all promotional efforts carefully to make sure that their advertisements are not offensive to women. Failure to recognize potential problems can cause later difficulties, such as product boycotts. Quebec, for example, now has a review board that monitors possibly offensive advertisements. In 1981, it presented its first "awards" for sexism. One award was conferred for a Sony and La Place stereo shop ad. This ad portrayed a big-busted woman, her nipples showing through her T-shirt, roller-skating while holding her Sony tape deck. The review jury found the promotion offensive as there was no connection between the woman and the product being advertised. Another "award" went to Proctor and Gamble for its 30-second Mr. Clean television commercial. In this ad, a little girl is shown cleaning up her brother's mess as he watches. The jury felt the company was reinforcing the old sex role stereotypes that housecleaning is women's work and that women should serve men.

Not only do advertisers have to be careful not to insult women, they must also avoid offending men. In one issue of its in-flight magazine, United Airlines innocently headlined a story about *Crocodile Dundee* star Paul Hogan. The title chosen was "Paul Hogan Camps It Up." Mr. Hogan's attorney was kind enough to inform United that *camps it up* is Australian slang for "flaunts his homosexuality."

Nike recently experienced some awkward moments in the United States when one of its television advertisements included people from various countries reportedly stating Nike's slogan—"Just do it"—in their native languages. However, one man, a Samburu tribesman, was really saying, "I don't want these, give me big shoes." Naturally, Nike's competition made sure people learned of the error. Nike admitted that their promotions staff did not really know what the natives were saying, but one suspects that Nike will be more careful in the future.

Many people who have traveled and can afford to stay at New York's Helmsley Palace Hotel know that the Taj Mahal is a mausoleum. However, that did not stop Leona Helmsley from approving a promotion that compared her hotel to the Taj Mahal. The headline stated, "In India It's the Taj Mahal. In New York It's the Helmsley Palace." It went on to proclaim, "Service and appointments fit for royalty—you—our guests."

In chapter 2, the problem of using inappropriate product and package colors was discussed. Colors can create promotional difficulties as well. The Singer Company, for example, found it necessary to halt an elaborate outdoor ad campaign when, just prior to the campaign's introduction, the company discovered that the background color, blue, was the local color representing death. Singer was fortunate that the error was discovered when it was. Because the company had hired local people to implement its promotional plan, the potential blunder was averted.

In terms of the visual content in promotion, the McDonnell Douglas Corporation experienced unexpected difficulties with a brochure that it planned to distribute to potential aircraft customers in India. The promotional material depicted turbaned men, but the photos were not well received. The company had used old *National Geographic* pictures and had overlooked the fact that the turbans were being worn by Pakistani men – not Indians.

The Marlboro man projects a strong masculine image in America and in Europe, but not everywhere. Attempts to use it were unsuccessful in Hong Kong, where urban consumers did not identify at all with horseback riding in the countryside. So Philip Morris quickly changed its ad to reflect a Hong Kong–style Marlboro man. He is still a virile cowboy, but he is younger, better dressed, and owns a truck as well as the land he's standing on.

Conducting business in a Communist country is especially tricky. A slip of the tongue or pen can prove fatal. Even the name of the country can cause troubles since the names given to some countries by the West are usually different than those used by the countries themselves. The failure to use the proper country name is often considered an insensitive or offensive act. For instance, the English-language catalog of a Swedish firm had to be changed because the catalog cited North Korea instead of the People's Republic of Korea. Similarly, another catalog used in China had to be altered when it listed North Vietnam. One company's promotional brochure stated that it had representatives in 100 countries and then proceeded to list Hong Kong as one of them. The problem? The People's Republic of China insists that Hong Kong is a colony rather than a country.

In another geographical blunder, United Airlines finally received permission in 1982 to initiate flights to Japan only to have its introductory campaign crash. United's public relations people in the United States tried to show customers the company's new route. Unfortunately, the map they used failed to include a major Japanese island. The Japanese are extremely sensitive about their territorial claims (and losses), and were highly offended by such a map. To them it showed ignorance or, perhaps worse, insensitivity. Although only a few copies of the map ever existed, the blunder made headline news in the second largest Japanese newspaper and drew a hasty apology from United. As United admitted, the mistake would never have happened had its staff in Tokyo had a chance to look at the map before its release.

Several firms have tried to use old, reliable promotional methods in countries where they simply do not work. Billboard advertisements are perfectly legal in most parts of the Middle East, for example, but this does not mean one should use them. Many companies have tried to employ billboards, but instead of advertising their product, they have merely exposed their lack of awareness of local weather conditions. In the hot, dry Middle Eastern environment, billboards often last less than two weeks.

Companies have even been known to promote their products using the wrong language. In Dubai, for example, only 10 percent of the population speaks Arabic. The remaining 90 percent of the people originate from Pakistan, India, Iran, or elsewhere. Several European and American firms, however, have assumed that all Middle Eastern countries are primarily populated by Arabic-speaking people and so have only promoted their products in Arabic. Similarly, *Time* magazine ran a Spanish-language ad in its Brazilian edition. Someone must have forgotten that they speak Portuguese in Brazil, not Spanish.

Misunderstandings

In many cases, the language of the promotional effort is correct, but the message is simply not effective. It is one thing to use the right language, but it is quite another to use it so that the intended message is properly communicated. As a classic illustration, consider the company that rented space on a wall beside the main road leading from the airport into Buenos Aires. The following message was placed on the wall: "With (brand name) you'd be there already." Just one slight problem existed: The message was misunderstood because it was placed on the wall of a cemetery. It may be easy to place a message in a slightly wrong location, but Amalie Refining was off by quite a few miles. One of its Spanish-language billboards somehow landed along the roadside in Knoxville, Tennessee.

A different type of locational error was committed by a firm at an international trade fair. In order to keep people out of a restricted area of its booth, the company displayed a sign depicting an open, flat hand with all fingers pointing up on a swinging door. To the company's surprise, the idea backfired. The local people interpreted the symbol to mean they should place their hands there and push open the door.

Symbols or logos have caused troubles for other companies as well. A U.S. firm marketing in Brazil found itself a bit embarrassed when it used a large deer as a sign for masculinity. The word *deer* is a Brazilian street name for "homosexual." Another company blundered in India when it used an owl in its promotional efforts. To an Indian, the owl is a symbol for bad luck, and indeed it proved to be just that for the firm.

Muslims in Dacca, Bangladesh, went on a rampage, ransacking shoe stores because they mistook the Thom McAn logo on some sandals for the Arabic characters for "Allah." They thought the Western company was denigrating their religion. Police were called in to stop the rioting, but at least one person was killed and fifty people were wounded before it was over.

A few years ago a Japanese steel firm, Sumitomo, introduced its specialty steel pipe in the U.S. market. Sumitomo used a Tokyo-based, Japanese agency to help develop its advertisements. The steel was named "Sumitomo *High Toughness*," and the name was promoted by the acronym SHT in bold letters. So bold, in fact, that the full-page ads run in trade journal were three-fourths filled with SHT. Located at the bottom of the page was a short message ending with the claim that the product "was made to match its name." The importance of local input simply cannot be overemphasized.

One laundry detergent company certainly wishes now that it had contacted a few locals before it initiated its promotional campaign in the Middle East. All of the company's advertisements pictured soiled clothes on the left, its box of soap in the middle, and clean clothes on the right. But because in that area of the world people tend to read from the right to the left, many potential customers interpreted the message to indicate the soap actually soiled the clothes.

Even if the proper words are used and positioned appropriately, problems can crop up due to incorrect intonation. Missionaries in Africa discovered this when someone finally informed them that the messages in their songs were being misunderstood. The words were correctly translated, but the tones and pitches used were not. For example, the Igbo people of Nigeria learned to sing the second verse of "Oh, Come All Ye Faithful." They were thought to be singing "Very God, begotten not created," but the actual meaning was "God's pig, which is never shared." Another hymn with the words "There is no sorrow in heaven" came out "There is no egg on the bicycle."

Care must be taken even when the consumers of a foreign market speak the same language. A British and U.S. joint venture proposal ran into serious difficulties, for example, when the U.S. firm requested that certain key points be "tabled." The British firm agreed and both parties prepared for negotiations. When the British team brought up for discussion those topics that had been tabled, both parties became highly irritated. In the United States "to table a motion" means to avoid discussing it, but in England the same phrase often means to bring the topic to the table for discussion. The Americans had inadvertently requested the exact opposite of what they had really wanted.

Similar problems were encountered by another U.S. company attempting to conduct business in Britain. The firm had effectively used the phrase "You can use no finer napkin at your dinner table" in the United States and, for economic reasons, decided to use the same commercials in England. After all, Britons do speak English. To a Briton, however, an American does not speak English but speaks "American," using different phrases and word meanings. Since the British word *napkin* or *nappy* actually means "diaper," the American firm was unknowingly advertising that "You could use no finer diaper at your dinner table." The ad was entertaining but could hardly be expected to boost sales.

American troubles with the English language are not limited to England, of course. One U.S. banker in Australia discovered this when he attended an important dinner given in his honor. He was invited to speak after the meal, but he certainly started off on the wrong foot by indicating that he was "full." The subsequent nervous laughter of the other diners suggested something was wrong, so he tried to clarify the situation by saying that he was "stuffed." One can imagine his astonishment when he learned that "full" implied being drunk, and "stuffed" suggested being involved in sexual intercourse.

Strategy

Often it is the promotional strategy that runs amuck and creates the promotional blunders. Whereas some companies have appeared culturally insensitive, others have actually blundered by going to the opposite extreme. They have tried to fake being local or have tried to appeal to local nationalistic pride. In 1963, for instance, Dow Breweries introduced a new beer in Quebec, Canada, called Kebec. The promotion incorporated the Canadian flag and attempted to evoke nationalistic pride. Dow's strategy backfired, however, when major local groups protested the "profane" use of "sacred" symbols. The campaign was halted within 15 days.

Similarly, when McDonald's used an illustration of Mexico's national flag on its place mats in 1988, the company drew the ire of local authorities. The Mexicans simply did not approve of ketchup being splattered all over one of its national symbols, so the place mats were confiscated. The offense, of course, was unintentional, but McDonald's apologized anyway.

Alka-Seltzer suffered a drastic downturn in its market share and profits when its new German owner, Bayer, decided to abandon Alka-Seltzer's traditional identity as a cure for blue-collar hangovers and tried to pitch the product as a remedy for young professional stress. Bayer eventually realized that it misunderstood the American market, so it switched back and recovered.

In another example of a company's misreading of the American market, a French beer company experienced difficulty trying to enter the U.S. market when it projected itself as American. Its decision to portray its imported beer as locally brewed was not a wise one because the American market was already flooded with local beers. The company, realizing its error, now does well promoting its beer as an import.

Products sell better when the promotions emphasize what the consumer considers important. Tires can be used as an example. Tire safety is stressed in Britain, durability and mileage are emphasized in the United States, and agile performance is considered important in Germany. Goodyear learned this lesson early and has been successful selling the same tire in all three markets using different messages.

Multinationals, therefore, must consider varying promotional tactics. Volvo has also applied this concept quite successfully. The company has emphasized economy, durability, and safety in America; status and leisure in France; performance in Germany; and safety in Switzerland. Price is considered to be a critical variable to Mexican consumers, but quality is of more importance to Venezuelans.

Test markets can be used to evaluate promotional campaigns, but results are not necessarily fail-safe. Puerto Rico is often used as a typical Latin American test market by U.S. companies. Although Puerto Rico is a convenient, almost barrier-free, Spanish-speaking market and thus an appealing test market, the natives of each Latin American country have their own unique tastes and preferences. Therefore, firms must realize that the success of a promotional strategy in Puerto Rico does not necessarily assure success in all Latin American countries. All that should be gleaned with confidence from a positive result in Puerto Rico is that the strategy is worth testing in the country under consideration. Major blunders have occurred when this second testing procedure was skipped. The managers of one company, for example, were so excited by the impressive results experienced in Puerto Rico that they shipped large quantities of their product, a hair fixer, to Argentina. Sales were practically nonexistent even though the commercials that had been so successful in Puerto Rico were used. Sales improved only after the local sales manager convinced the company to alter the ads and direct them towards a more European-type customer.

Unilever experienced a somewhat unique type of promotional problem. The company marketed a popular detergent, Radion, in Germany. It also sold the same basic product in Austria but marketed it under a different brand name. Because Germans and Austrians both speak German and are often exposed to each other's media, consumers in each country were being introduced to what they thought were competitive products. Since the promotional campaigns developed for one country easily reached the consumers in the other country, a more efficient and effective marketing strategy would have been to use the same brand name in both countries. Had this occurred, the promotional overlap would have reinforced their efforts and helped sales.

One fairly common American practice is that of utilizing the same promotional strategy for all domestic subsidiaries. Promotional budgets are often based on a fixed-percentage-of-sales basis. This strategy often works well with domestic ventures but usually proves foolish when it is attempted for overseas subsidiaries as well. U.S. companies that try to force such standardization are often asking their foreign managers to do the impossible. For one thing, some types of media are not legally available. In many countries, no television advertisements are permitted. This alone makes a U.S.-style promotional budget unfeasible. A second problem is one of scale. The use of a standard percentage of sales may be appropriate for large, domestic subsidiaries, but for small foreign subsidiaries, 10 percent may not support a single promotional campaign. Several companies have attempted standardized promotional budgets, but most have now realized that each market provides different opportunities and challenges at different cost structures. A better strategy is to standardize the methods used to analyze opportunities and the methods used to develop local promotional budgets. Subsidiaries can then be urged to follow these established methods during the development of their own promotional budgets.

Cultural Differences

Dozens of blunders have been made by firms that failed to study local customs carefully. As one example, consider the public display of physical contact between members of opposite sexes. In many countries, this is totally unacceptable and offensive. Thailand is one of these countries. A firm trying to introduce its mouthwash there, however, was not aware of this norm and promoted its product through an ad that displayed a young couple holding hands. By changing the advertisement to feature two women, the commercials were deemed acceptable and no longer offensive to the Thais.

Asian Indians found a BiNoca Talc ad disturbing even though the woman in the advertisement was wearing a body stocking. The promotion, appearing in many of the major local newspapers, featured an attractive but apparently nude young woman lavishly splashing herself with BiNoca's talcum powder. Strategic portions of her body were carefully covered with the slogan "Don't go wild – just enough is all you need of BiNoca Talc." The public, however, was not prepared for the ad's use of the female form and found the ads extremely indecent.

In other countries, such exposure is not deemed to be offensive. In fact, the French, more than many nationalities, accept commercials that feature a great deal of the female body.

To some ethnic groups, the display of certain seemingly innocuous parts of the body proves to be offensive. One American shoe manufacturer promoted its product through photos of bare feet. Although considered a harmless advertisement by many, the photos were introduced in Southeast Asia where exposure of the foot is considered an insult.

Mountain Bell experienced a similar problem when one of its promotional photos depicted an executive talking on the telephone with his feet propped up on his desk. The photos, seen by Middle and Far Easterners, were considered to be in poor taste. To them, the display of the sole of the foot or shoe is a terrible insult.

Another American firm trying to do business in Saudi Arabia ran into problems with some advertising art work. The ad pictured a man's fist clenching a rock. This design was intended to symbolize the company's solid position as a manufacturer of rock-crushing equipment. Unfortunately, the upward position of the hand symbolized a motion considered very offensive by the Saudis. Again, local input can be vital in avoiding blunders. Many promotional errors could have been averted had this warning been heeded.

Another well-known promotional blunder occurred in Quebec. In this instance, a manufacturer of canned fish ran advertisements in the local newspapers that depicted a woman in shorts playing golf with a man. The caption explained that a woman could go golfing with her husband in the afternoon and still get home in time to serve a great dinner of canned fish that same evening. The entire promotional effort was off-target. Women did not wear shorts on local golf courses and did not usually golf with men. Furthermore, regardless of how much preparation time was available, women would not have considered serving canned fish for dinner, especially as the main course. The company seems to have completely neglected to consider local customs, and obviously the product failed.

Pepsodent reportedly tried to sell its toothpaste in regions of Southeast Asia through a promotion which stressed that the toothpaste helped enhance white teeth. In this area, where some local people deliberately chewed betel nut in order to achieve the social prestige of darkly stained teeth, such an ad was understandably less than effective. Many also viewed the slogan "Wonder where the yellow went" as a racial slur.

A marketer of eyeglasses promoted his spectacles in Thailand using commercials that featured animals wearing glasses. This was an unfortunate decision, however, since animals there are considered a low life form, and it is beneath humans to wear anything worn by an animal.

The failure of firms to consider specialized aspects of local religions has also created a number of difficulties. Companies have encountered problems in Asia when they incorporated pictures of Buddha in their promotions. Religious ties are strong in this area, and the use of local religious symbols in advertising is strongly resented – especially when words are deliberately or even accidentally printed across the picture of Buddha. One company was nearly burned to the ground when it ignorantly tried such a strategy. The seemingly minor incident led to a major international political conflict remembered for years.

Another religious-type blunder occurred when a refrigerator manufacturer ran an ad picturing a refrigerator that contained a centrally placed chunk of ham. The typical refrigerator advertisement often features a refrigerator full of delicious food, and because these photos are difficult to take, the photos are generally used in as many places as possible. This company used its stock photo one place too many, though, when it appeared in the Middle East where Muslims do not eat ham. Locals considered the ad to be both insensitive and unappealing.

An entertainment promoter also encountered difficulties when he failed to recognize one of the Muslim mores. He had booked singer Anita Sarawak in Singapore, and during her performance, encouraged her to hold her pet dog while singing "Me and You and a Dog Named Boo." This gimmick had worked well in other countries but caused a major commotion in Singapore. Plans for subsequent taped broadcasts of the show were cancelled, all because of the dog. According to Islamic beliefs, dogs are dirty and should not be shown or kept as pets.

Saudi Arabia nearly restricted an airline from initiating flights when the company authorized "normal" newspaper advertisements. The ads featured attractive hostesses serving champagne to the happy airline passengers. Because alcohol is illegal and unveiled women are not permitted to mix with men in Saudi Arabia, the photo was viewed as an attempt to alter religious customs.

Since successful advertisements usually involve cultural assumptions, using the same commercial in more than one country can be dangerous. Cosmetics firms in the United States, for example, often pitch their messages to flatter the American woman's ego by telling her how attractive she is or will be if she uses their products. Similar commercials have been introduced in France and have failed. French women do not identify themselves as being ultraglamorous nor do they believe that they can be. Often they do not even realize that the commercial is aimed at them, and so they simply assume that the message must be intended for a rare few.

A major cereal company reportedly experienced problems with its breakfast food commercials when it implemented a promotional strategy in Britain similar to the one used in America. The American ads often featured children and aimed the messages towards them. Even the packages pictured the typical freckled, red-haired American kid. The British, however, resented both the use of the children in the promotion and the company's attempt to influence children. They considered it improper to aim a sales pitch at a child and forced the firm to create totally new commercials directed toward adults. Although the company originally named in the report now denies that it was involved, the conclusion remains the same: Awareness of local cultural norms is critical.

Acceptable methods of information presentation also vary from culture to culture. In the Far East, for example, a person should not try to make the other "lose face." But to be taken seriously in Italy, a person must try to win the argument. A person speaking precisely will be taken literally in Switzerland. The British prefer a much "softer sell" than the Germans.

In advertising as in production, choosing a color is another important consideration. At least two different firms encountered problems in their Hong Kong marketing efforts when they decided to use green hats in commercials. One company attempted to sell its beer using the message that the beer was so good that even the Irish like it. The Irishman, of course, wore a green hat while drinking his beer. The other firm marketed cleaning agents and in its commercial featured individuals tossing hats at a male model. A green hat eventually landed on the man. In both cases, the color chosen was not appropriate; the green hat is a Chinese symbol used to identify a man as a cuckold. Understandably, consumers avoided both products.

As Guinness Stout can attest, Hong Kong has been the site of more than one unexpected turn of events. This firm's thick brew, considered especially well suited for virile men of the British empire, had somehow achieved a reputation in Hong Kong for being an excellent drink for women during pregnancy or menstrual periods. Consequently, when the drink was promoted in Hong Kong as one for men, it elicited much laughter. Any man ordering it was likely to be asked if it was his "time of the month."

Another unusual problem occurred in Peru when a laundry detergent containing stain-removing enzymes was introduced through a cartoon depicting large-mouthed enzymes eating the dirt off clothes. Although sales levels were initially good, they quickly dropped off. A local Peruvian custom was at the bottom of the company's problem. Peruvian women believed that they must boil their clothes to kill the germs, and the voracious cartoon creatures in the ad reinforced this belief. However, because the boiling destroyed the enzymes, the detergent was boiled to a useless state and did not perform as advertised. As a result, since the product was not as effective as expected, the women only used it once.

Not all companies find that their products are being used correctly, but sometimes unusual uses do not hurt sales. Gervais Danone, for example, was able to turn the tables on a potential problem. The company, finding that the Mexicans had little interest in its products, decided to alter its promotional strategy. It found that it was eventually able to interest the adults in using its cheeses for butter and its Petite Swisse, a creamy whipped cheese, as a good snack for the children.

The Latin Market in the United States   Not all cultural problems occur outside the multinational company's home country. For example, a significant Latino market exists in the United States, and it is becoming increasingly obvious that companies need to be aware of Latino culture. Sometimes it is even worthwhile to develop separate and special promotional campaigns aimed at this market. Colgate Palmolive, for example, has been able to promote its toothpaste effectively within the Hispanic community through ads that place less emphasis on health and more emphasis on appearance. Not all companies are so successful, however. Several examples of misses or near misses in promotional efforts follow.

Braniff Airlines produced one infamous advertisement that was broadcast in Spanish over several U.S. radio stations. Unfortunately, the speaker unintentionally encouraged travelers to "fly naked" when the message actually was intended to describe the leather seats in Braniff airplanes. Someone had written the message correctly using *en cuero* for "in leather." But *en cueros* means "naked" in Spanish, and the *s* is not pronounced. Therefore, both words sound the same. So while the message was technically correctly translated, the problem would not have arisen had a native Spanish-speaking person looked over the ad first.

A telephone company tried to incorporate a Latino flavor in its commercial by employing Puerto Rican actors. In the ad, the wife said to her husband, "Run downstairs and phone Mary. Tell her we'll be a little late." This commercial contained two major cultural errors: in a traditional household, Latino wives would seldom dare order their husbands around, and almost no spouse would feel it necessary to phone to warn of tardiness.

Coors commercials promoting the slogan "Taste the high country" featured people enjoying Coors beer and life in the Rocky Mountains. This approach, very effective with Anglo-Americans, did not appeal to Mexican-Americans who could not identify with mountain life. Therefore, the Spanish language ads were modified. The mountains were identified as a good source of beer, but one did not necessarily need to live in the mountains to enjoy the beer or to be happy. The new slogan, in its English version, became "Take the beer from the high country and bring it to your high country – wherever it may be."

McDonald's has used "Hispanic ads" in several Spanish-speaking markets within the United States. However, these same ads proved unsuccessful when introduced in Puerto Rico. Apparently Puerto Rican consumers deemed them "too Mexican," so separate ads had to be developed.

On the other hand, Johnson and Johnson was fortunate and discovered a potential cultural blunder in time to correct it. The firm was all set to promote its disposable diapers through advertisements that contained references to a mother's wet lap and a father's being dry when it was uncovered that such phrases bore indelicate sexual references to Hispanic consumers. This discovery was fortunate since such an ad would have created a great deal of embarrassment for the company.

Pedro Domecq wines also averted a mishap when it was about to use the slogan "the art of simpatico drinking" to promote Spanish wines. A U.S. advertising agency had created the slogan, which was intended to tie together the Spanish wine and the favorable U.S. translation and use of the word *simpatico*. However, the Spanish do not use the word with the same connotation. The correct Spanish usage is "El es muy *simpatico*" (he is very likable, agreeable, genial). Since, in Spanish, *simpatico* always refers to a person and never to a drink, the promotional campaign would have seemed foolish to the Spanish-speaking community. Fortunately, some Spanish-speaking managers from Pedro Domecq revealed this error in time.

PRICING

Setting an appropriate price for a product is often much more difficult than it appears. If only one insignificant detail of the pricing procedure is overlooked or misjudged, major troubles can develop for the firm.

Consider the experience of a company trying to market cans of luncheon meat. In order to beat the prices of its competitors, the firm slightly cut its prices by rounding them off to easy-to-record, even numbers. The customary prices of the competitors' products were a bit higher, and to the disappointment of the company, customers seemed quite willing to pay the minor extra charge. A local business practice was actually involved in this mishap. Local retail outlets usually operated on very small profit margins. These retailers found that their customers would not request the small change due when purchasing the fractionally higher priced can of meat. Naturally, in order to keep their "tip," the retailers heavily promoted the competition. It took the firm over six months to readjust its price and begin selling its product again.

Sometimes the price set is simply too high. In the 1960s, for example, an American food company attempted to sell its soup at a price of 80 cents per can. Because most French housewives considered soup to be a minor appetizer, they were unwilling to spend the required amount of money, and consequently, the soup did not sell well. The Delacre line of luxury biscuits promoted under the Pepperidge Farm label encountered similar problems when it was introduced in the United States. The biscuits did not sell well until the British firm Peek Freanline introduced them at a much lower price. Products are not prized in all countries, so what some may be willing to pay highly for, others may not. In a foreign environment, any assumption concerning a product's "special value" is dangerous. Unless the market is clearly established, the implementation of a high pricing strategy is not likely to achieve high sales volumes.

In the early 1960s, Princess Housewares experienced pricing difficulties in the German marketplace. During that period in Germany, small appliances were generally distributed to retail outlets through independent wholesalers. However, department stores, mail order houses, and discount outlets were gaining popularity. Due to their size, these large retailers were able to obtain products at lower prices and could market goods at very competitive prices. Consequently, resale price maintenance became very difficult. In order to protect the small retailers' margins, Princess Housewares decided to enforce undiscounted prices. Thus, the company eventually found itself at a competitive disadvantage when selling to the large retailers and was greatly hurt by its failure to accept this new up-and-coming retail trend. Similar marketing trends in the United States a few years earlier should have signaled the increasing importance of large retail outlets.

Price negotiation can also prove to be a tricky undertaking. If the company negotiators are unaware of local customs, inappropriate prices are quite likely to result. This risk is best illustrated by examining the negotiation process involving American and Japanese managers. American managers are accustomed to pressure decision making and are often given the authority to make final decisions. Japanese managers, on the other hand, prefer to negotiate more slowly, tend to make decisions by group consensus, and always politely listen to everyone in their group before reaching an official decision. Because Americans are generally unaware of these tendencies, they have often created problems for themselves.

A typical situation involves an American negotiating with Japanese managers in order to buy or sell some product or service. The American, often anxious to complete the deal, tends (in the eyes of the Japanese) to rush the negotiation process. All too often, when the time for price discussion arrives, the American will quickly suggest a price. Being used to the give-and-take of negotiating, the American usually does not make the best possible offer at the start nor necessarily expects it to be accepted. Here is where the troubles arise. When people hesitate, an American tends to assume that the price mentioned is an unacceptable one. Therefore, an American will sometimes hastily improve the offer even before it is rejected or the process is unsuccessfully terminated. But the American negotiating with Japanese managers may commit a blunder by quickly altering the price.

This has happened on numerous occasions, but in at least one reported case, an American raised the price he was willing to pay three times after the Japanese were prepared to accept. Unaware of Japanese customs, he did not realize that the hesitation and discussion between the Japanese (in Japanese, of course) were not a result of unhappiness over the price quoted. With each higher price offer, the Japanese negotiators expressed amazement (in Japanese) but then proceeded to check out their colleagues' opinions. This delay only unwittingly encouraged the American to offer even more.

Many companies that have been able to buy or sell merchandise at the right prices have occasionally quoted the prices forgetting that exchange rates fluctuate. Because totally accurate exchange rate forecasting is not possible, some mistakes have been made. The direction of currency movement is fairly predictable, though, and should be considered when a company prices a contract for future payment.

Similarly, in most countries, inflation is fairly predictable. The failure to analyze inflationary factors has hurt a number of companies. A German company, for example, agreed to a $163 million Algerian construction contract. The price set was fair enough at the time of the commitment, but costs rose dramatically during the life of the contract. Unfortunately, the firm had failed to include protective price escalators in the original contract. Additionally, it soon discovered that payments were made in the local Algerian currency which had also declined in value. This double-edged sword cut out all the company's expected profits and cost the firm millions of dollars.

Credit, another price-related variable, is often critical to the marketing strategy. Although the product might be appropriately priced, it may not sell if credit terms are unacceptable. Consider a multinational firm that had carefully test-marketed its specially modified washing machines and concluded that they would sell well in Latin America. Sales were slow even though a large shipment had been made available. Eventually the firm discovered the trouble: local competitors were making their sales on credit. Apparently those participating in the market test had assumed that credit would be made available since it was the local business practice. So, when asked during the test if they would buy, they replied "yes." Only after they discovered that no credit would be provided did they change their minds and decide not to purchase the product. In light of these examples, it should be clear that all aspects of pricing and selling strategies must be considered carefully.

SUMMARY

This chapter has introduced a number of problems encountered when companies attempted to promote products in international markets. Blunders have been made in all types of media and for a wide variety of reasons. Both simple and complex misunderstandings have led to promotion difficulties. Sometimes mistakes arose from human error or the use of culturally insensitive persons. On occasion, an entire promotional strategy has proved foolish. In many cases, the blunders were simply the result of the company's failure to understand cultural differences, some basic but some more subtle. A few problems encountered were because of pricing errors. With so many different kinds of potential blunders, it is easy to believe that every promotional task imaginable has been bungled at one time or another by someone, someplace.

5
TRANSLATION

Translation errors are the cause of the greatest number and variety of blunders in international business. There are three basic categories of translation errors: simple carelessness, multiple-meaning words, and idioms. All three types are described and discussed in this chapter.

CARELESSNESS

The most prevalent type of translation blunder is merely the careless rendering of a promotional message into another language. Obviously, these mistakes can often result in an embarrassing or damaging situation, and thus directly injure sales.

Consider, for example, a food company that did indeed make a "big mistake" when it advertised its giant burrito as a "burrada." The colloquial meaning of the word *burrada* is "big mistake." Spanish language translations seem to prove treacherous for companies. One Spanish ad promoted Budweiser as the "Queen of Beers," a slight variation on the company's usual "King of Beers" slogan. Another Spanish language blunder occurred when an advertisement for Bud Lite beer was translated into Spanish as "Filling, less delicious" rather than "Delicious, less filling."

In an advertisement that recently ran in New York, Acura proudly proclaimed, "The Legend and Integra, cars that break tradition, *now* your bank account." Obviously Acura intended to say "not" rather than "now," but to some consumers the error may have had an accidental ring of truth to it.

An American in Michigan got so upset with the success of Japanese automakers that he decided to make and sell T-shirts displaying a message that was supposed to say, in both English and Japanese, "Buy American made." Naturally, he had no trouble with the English, but the Japanese translation came out as "Buy an American maid."

When Pope John Paul II visited Miami several years ago, a local businessman thought he would profit by printing messages on T-shirts declaring in Spanish, "I saw the Pope." He earned more laughs than money, though. The shirts were printed with "La Papa" rather than "El Papa" and, therefore, proclaimed that the wearer had seen "the potato."

A toy bear, made in Taiwan, "sang" Christmas carols in English. One song, though, didn't quite come out correctly: It was "Oh Little Town of Birmingham." It helps to know the story.

One company in Taiwan tried to sell diet food to expatriates living there. The company urged consumers to buy its product to add "roughage" to their systems. How much roughage should a person consume? Well, the instructions claimed that one should eat it until "your tool floats." Do you suppose they meant "stool"?

An automobile manufacturer promoted its product in an English-speaking market by declaring that its product "topped them all." This may have been so, but the French Canadians would not have known. When the product was introduced, the phrase was mistranslated in French. The result: The company actually boasted that its cars were "topped by them all." Another American manufacturer in the auto industry advertised its car battery as "highly rated." Unfortunately, when the company introduced its product in Venezuela, the battery was described as "highly overrated." Here again the company had used a thoughtless translation of a key promotional phrase. Consequently, sales did not boom in either case.

Kentucky Fried Chicken consistently has done very well overseas. However, even a good company can make mistakes. KFC experienced real problems when the phrase "finger lickin' good" came out in Chinese as "eat your fingers off." Likewise, Eastern Airlines translated its "We earn our wings daily" message into Spanish in such a way that the translated message implied that the airline's passengers often ended up dead. This, naturally, did not help Eastern's struggle to avoid bankruptcy. And the Olfa Corporation, a Japanese manufacturer, sold knives in America with a very interesting warning on the package: "Caution: Blade extremely sharp! Keep out of children."

A Canadian importer of Turkish shirts destined for Quebec used a dictionary to help him translate the label "Made in Turkey." Unfortunately, his translated message, "Fabriqué en Dinde," reflected his limited knowledge of French – *dinde* is the bird, *Turquie* is the country.

Careless translations can prove to be humorous to the consumer and/or embarrassing to the firm. Consider, for example, the experience of the Otis Engineering Corporation when it participated in an exhibition held in Moscow. Initially, the company's representatives could not discern why its display won Soviet snickers as well as praise. Much to their disappointment and embarrassment, it was discovered that a careless translator had rendered a sign that identified "completion equipment" as "equipment for orgasms."

On the opposite side of the globe, another firm was experiencing the headaches caused by a poor translator. In this case, a Mexican magazine promotion for an American brand shirt carried a message stating the exact opposite of what had originally been intended. The advertisement, instead of declaring, "When I used this shirt, I felt good," read, "Until I used this shirt, I felt good."

The Frank Perdue Company is well known for its catchy messages promoting its chicken products. At least one of its popular slogans, though, was not translated very well. The message, declaring approximately that "It takes a tough man to make a tender chicken," somehow came out closer to "It takes a sexually excited man to make a chick affectionate."

Many a small business has thwarted its own efforts through the use of poor translation. For example, one business person, trying to save a bit of money, hired an Indonesian exchange student to translate the instruction manual of a computer destined for Jakarta. Not surprisingly, the student did not understand computer terminology, so the computer "software" was translated as "underwear." The manual must have provided interesting reading to those who purchased the computer.

In efforts to attract tourists and foreign business people, some small businesses have created rather funny situations. For instance, a department store in Thailand posted a sign that read, "Visit our bargain basement one flight up." Another misguided individual in Thailand tried to attract business with a sign asking, "Would you like to ride on your ass?" And in Japan, an interesting but misleading translation showed up on a sign in a Japanese garden. The posted sign read, "Japanese garden is the mental home of the Japanese."

A number of years ago American businessmen reported seeing a sign in a Tokyo hotel that read, "You are respectfully requested to take advantage of the chambermaids." The translation is probably misleading, but not as dangerous as the faulty translations of some equipment-handling instructions that have led to the injury and death of several construction employees in the Middle East.

An interesting sign in Czechoslovakia read, "Take one of our horse-driven tours. We guarantee no miscarriages." That, however, probably didn't generate as much interest as the sign in a French shop window that read, "We sell dresses for street walking." It is probably best to assume that both signs were the result of translation errors.

One dentist in Hong Kong apparently advertised, "Teeth extracted by the latest Methodists." A more startling sign, however, showed up in the window of a tailor in Jordan. The sign advised the following: "Order you summers suit. Because if big rush we will execute customers in strict rotation."

A company in Taiwan wished to help foreigners communicate more effectively, so it advertised its expertise in a brochure. The text read, in part, that "communication was a new challenge," and that the firm could "translet [sic] your idea clearly . . . to people who have no lot of time to sit or listen." Obviously, the firm needed to hire someone to help it improve its own communication skills.

A Chinese restaurant in Virginia ran an ad in a local newspaper with a line of Chinese characters printed upside down. That is an understandable mistake, but the restaurant compounded this mistake in a subsequent ad that tried to explain the error. The characters were right side up in the second ad, but in reverse order. There is no report as to how the third version looked.

Business people in Mexico City report that a hotel there proclaimed, "The manager has personally passed all the water served here." Others report a Moscow hotel sign that read, "If this is your first visit to the USSR, you are welcome to it." A Swiss restaurant boasted, "Our wines leave you nothing to hope for," and a bathroom sign in Finland suggested, "To stop the drip, turn cock to right."

A firm in the Middle East was able to attract attention, but not exactly the kind for which it had hoped. It seems that a Saudi Arabian laundry had posted, in English, a list of its cleaning prices. It was not its prices, though, that were attracting people. The company had used a poor translator, and among the many spelling errors on the poster was the omission of the letter *r* in "lady's shirt." One can imagine the customers' reactions. Another laundry, this time a hotel laundry in Tokyo, experienced a similarly embarrassing situation. The hotel's instructions, translated into English, stated, "The flattening of underwear with pressure is the job of the chambermaid. To get it done, turn her on." One suspects that the message was literally translated, but obviously it is not to be taken this way. It is easy, therefore, to understand the importance of an accurate translation and the possible negative results of a poor translation.

One of the more unusual errors made by a small business occurred in Kowloon. A sign in the hotel read, "It is forbidden to steal hotel towels, please if you are not person to do such is please not to read notice." What one can assume from this is that someone tried to communicate in another language, but with a bit of difficulty.

Translation blunders seem to occur everywhere but for now consider only one specific location – Quebec. Quebec has been the site of a number of corporate blunders, most of them due to simple carelessness. There is no reason, for example, for a firm to have used the words *lavement d'auto* (car enema) instead of the correct *lavage d'auto* (car wash), but one firm did.

Another company boasted of *lait frais usagé* (used fresh milk) when it meant to brag of *lait frais employé* (fresh milk used). The terrific pens of one firm were promoted as *terrifiantes* (terrifying) instead. Indeed, such a poor translation is terrifying. One company, intending to report that its appliance would use any kind of electrical current, actually stated that the appliance wears out any kind of liquid. And imagine how one company felt when its product to reduce heartburn was advertised as one that reduced warmth of heart. Another unfortunate firm claimed that its product was a stumbling block to success when it really wanted to claim that its product provided a stepping stone to success.

The omission of an accent mark created difficulties for at least one company. An American firm hoped to surprise its Mexican-based employees with a New Year's Eve party. Preparations were complete, including balloons with printed slogans (in Spanish) declaring "Happy New Year." However, the accent mark over the *n* in *año* was left off. Without the mark, the word read *ano* (anus, in Spanish). Happy New Anus? As expected, the balloons came down before midnight.

All of these blunders point out that even the smallest translation error can greatly affect the intended message and the market's reaction to that message. Occasionally it may only be one seemingly insignificant letter that can change the entire context of the copy. Consider one unfortunate international corporation that had its annual report translated into Spanish. In the sentence "Our vast enterprise achieved record sales," the word *vast* was translated into *basto*. The actual Spanish word is *vasto*, but people often become confused because the letters *b* and *v* are pronounced similarly. Due to this error in translation, however, the entire meaning of the sentence was modified to "Our crude and uncultured enterprise achieved record sales."

MULTIPLE MEANINGS

The second category of translation blunders involves translated messages that can convey more than one meaning. The trials and tribulations experienced by the Parker Pen Company serve as an excellent illustration of how an innocent translation of a multiple-meaning word or phrase can create complex promotion problems. In its advertisements destined for Latin America, Parker had hoped to use the word *bola* to describe its ballpoint pen. However, it was discovered that the word conveys different meanings in different Latin countries. To some, "bola" conveys the intended meaning of "ball," while in another country, the translation means "revolution." "Bola" represents an obscenity in a third country, and in yet another, it means a "lie" or "fabrication." Luckily, the firm was able to uncover this translation problem before it ever became a blunder.

The company, however, was not so fortunate when it tried to introduce its fountain pens in some parts of Latin America. The Parker Pen Company had developed and promoted in the United States one of the first truly reliable fountain pens. A person could carry the pen in a shirt pocket without having to worry about the possibility of embarrassing ink stains. The advertisements (and the pens) performed so well that the Parker Pen became quite well known. Eventually, the promotion was shortened to convey that Parker Pens avoid embarrassment. Because this condensed version of the promotional slogan was so successful over time, the older expanded message was taken for granted and basically forgotten. Later, when the firm decided to enter the Latin American market, it merely translated the same condensed promotional slogan then being used in the United States: "Avoid embarrassment – use Parker Pens." The company even posted metal signs featuring this short message on the buildings in which its pens were sold, but the results of the company's promotional efforts were not as anticipated. What had gone wrong? The company had promoted a slogan that contained a multiple-meaning word. The Spanish word for "embarrassment" was also used to indicate pregnancy, so the Parker Pen Company was unknowingly promoting its pens as contraceptives.[5]

An American toothpaste manufacturer also experienced pains with its "pregnancy." The company promised its customers that they would be more "interesting" if they used the firm's toothpaste. What the advertising coordinators did not realize, however, was that in some Latin American countries the word *interesting* is another euphemism for "pregnant."

Continuing with problems of pregnancy, consider the case of a free-lance Arabic translator who translated an American computer manual into his native language. When confronted with the terms *dummy* and *load*, specialized electronics terms, he consulted his dictionary and found the equivalents for "dummy" and "load." When he put these two together, he produced the Arabic term for "false pregnancy."

Wendy's was saved from committing two separate blunders in Germany by advertising agency staff members. In one case, Wendy's wanted to promote its "old-fashioned" qualities. A literal translation, however, would have resulted in the company promoting itself as "outdated." In another example, Wendy's wanted to emphasize that its hamburgers could be prepared 256 ways. The problem? The German word Wendy's wanted to use for *ways* usually meant "roads" or "highways." Although such errors may sometimes entertain the public, it is certainly preferable to catch these mistakes before they confuse the consumer or embarrass the company. Consider the following translation blunders due to multiple meanings.

First, the Spanish certainly enjoyed a good laugh when Chrysler Corporation tried to promote its successful U.S. slogan, "Dart is power." It seems that the translated version of this message implied that drivers of the car needed the sexual vigor that the Dart would supply. Second, a Swedish company purchased the well-known vacuum cleaner manufacturer, Electrolux. New ads were developed for the American market proclaiming that "Electrolux sucks better." Obviously, the firm was not attuned to some common American slang. Third, in Thailand, a bar located close to some trees and buildings that blocked out the hot sun innocently advertised itself as "the shadiest bar in Bangkok."

These double-meaning translation errors embarrass the firms involved. One company caught in this situation was granted the dubious distinction of winning *Playboy* magazine's annual "Booby-Boo-Boo Award." Apparently when Hunt-Wesson introduced the Big John family brand in Canada it experienced a bit of difficulty with the French translation. The name, translated as *Gros Jos*, also turned out to be a colloquial French expression that denoted a woman with large breasts. In this case the company was fortunate. Its sales were not badly hurt for a number of men wanted to order the Gros Jos.

Hunt-Wesson has not been the only company to find itself in such a humorous position. A U.S. airline that proudly advertised swank "rendezvous lounges" aboard its Boeing 747 jets may have wished that its promotion had never reached Brazil. After advertising these accommodations, the company belatedly learned that *rendez-vous* in Portuguese means a room that is rented out for prostitution. Although the promotion was successful in attracting attention, sales did not increase. No Brazilian wanted to be seen getting on or off the airline's plane. Here again, a company's failure to understand all of the meanings and implications of the translated message was responsible for its subsequent promotion difficulties.

Several major tobacco companies have also experienced the pitfall of a double meaning. These firms advertised "low-tar" cigarettes in Spanish-speaking countries but misused the word *brea*. *Brea* literally translates to "tar," but it is the type of tar used for paving streets. Care for a "low-asphalt" cigarette, anyone?

A promotional slogan used by the General Motors Corporation serves as another example of a humorous double-meaning translation blunder. The company had intended to convey to its Belgian consumers that the car being promoted had a "body by Fisher," but the phrase was interpreted in Flemish as "corpse by Fisher."

A sign in a Japanese museum advised patrons in English to "Please refrain from taking photographs and reproducing." Literal translations are risky. It is probably just as well that most people in English-speaking countries do not know that the motto for Tokyo Gas and Electric is "My life, my gas."

Translated words may often mean about the same thing, but they may not elicit the same feelings. As an example, "As smooth as a baby's bottom" was translated in Japanese to "As smooth as a baby's ass." Translators should convey the intended mood even if this means forgoing a literal translation and using alternate wording instead.

American cooks understand what is meant by *tomato paste,* but how does one translate this into Arabic? The closest translation is something like "tomato glue." Thus, translators have had to use the Arabic words for "tomato puree." Sounds a bit more appetizing, doesn't it?

Sometimes someone in a company simply forgets that words have well-known double meanings. One firm, for example, experienced trouble conducting market research. It requested information regarding the annual German production of washers. The firm was actually seeking data on washing machines, but instead received material on the production of flat metal discs (also known as washers). Here the translation problem was not so much with the translated word or the translator, but with the original word.

Adolph Coors Co. hired an agency to develop promotional material for its Coors Light beer that would appeal to Hispanics in the United States. The copywriter tried to translate the phrase "Turn it loose" into Spanish, but unfortunately used words that meant "Drink Coors and get diarrhea." The commercial received a lot of attention but not the kind for which Coors had hoped.

Tropicana tried to sell its orange juice in Miami claiming that it was "jugo de China." *China* means "orange" to Puerto Ricans, but not to the Cubans in Miami. Thus, the Cubans thought that it was "juice from China" and were not very interested in the product.

Miami is frequently the site of linguistic problems. Several different cultures coexist there with people speaking different languages – or sometimes the same one with different meanings. Take the word *bichos,* for example. It means "bugs" to Mexicans, but the word denotes a man's private parts to Puerto Ricans. Therefore, the insecticide company's posters guaranteeing that its products will kill all "bichos" was not very successful in some parts of Miami.

One final example of the troublesome multiple-meaning word involves the banking industry. An American bank was given a 30-day option on the purchase of a Middle Eastern bank. During the final negotiations, an unfortunate buyer proposed in French that the loans be put into an escrow account. The local sellers, quite humiliated and shocked, quickly left the room shouting, "A reserve for cheating? Never!" The misunderstanding stemmed from the word *escrow,* which when translated into French means "a gyp." Quite upset, the sellers decided to find another interested party willing to purchase the bank.

From the examples, it is clear that translations play a key role in all aspects of international business, and that accuracy is of utmost importance. A company can be hurt greatly by one simple faulty translation.

IDIOMS

Having discussed not only those errors resulting from careless translation but also those due to multiple meanings, consider now the third type of blunder: those made during the translation of idioms and expressions. Because of the unique aspect of the idiomatic expressions that characterize every language, this is often the most difficult area. The following examples have been chosen as illustrations.

Most firms realize it takes more than a bilingual dictionary to translate commercial messages and their intended meanings. However, a few firms have used the simplest, most literal translations for their promotions, and as a result have found themselves promoting something other than what they had thought. An American company, for instance, advertised its product to a Spanish audience by exclaiming that anyone who didn't wear its brand of hosiery just "wouldn't have a leg to stand on." But when the copy was translated the firm actually declared that the wearer would "only have one leg."

Almost everyone is familiar with the Pepsi-Cola advertising slogan "Come alive with Pepsi." Reportedly, when the campaign was introduced in Germany, the company was forced to revise the ad because it discovered that the German translation of "Come alive" was "Come out of the grave." And in Asia, the same phrase translated to "Bring your ancestors back from the dead." The intended meaning of this famous slogan was definitely lost somewhere in these two translations.[6]

Another case of a troublesome literal translation occurred in French-speaking Quebec. The point-of-sale campaign of a laundry soap company stressed the extra-strong cleaning powers of its product and its effectiveness at washing the especially dirty parts of the wash, *les parts de sale*. When the soap sales declined, the company investigated and discovered that this phrase is comparable to the American slang phrase "private parts."

The English expression *touch-toe* was responsible for a blunder made by a manufacturer of dental equipment. In a brochure written for the Soviet market, the company featured the "touch-toe" control of its dental chair movement. The translator, however, rendered the description of this feature in such a way that the Russians thought that the dentist had to be barefooted in order to operate the equipment.

Several other brief examples of mistranslated English idioms or expressions illustrate how often these blunders have been made. One European firm certainly missed the point when it translated the expression "Out of sight, out of mind" as "Invisible things are insane" in Thailand. There is also the story of the phrase "The spirit is willing, but the flesh is weak" being translated to "The liquor is holding out all right, but the meat has spoiled." And consider, finally, a translation of the name for Schweppes Tonic Water to the Italian *il water*. The copy was speedily dehydrated to Schweppes Tonica because "il water" idiomatically indicates a bathroom.

If anything is to be learned from these examples, it is the necessity for caution in the translation and interpretation of intended messages. Exact wording should not always be translated literally. This can be most appropriately demonstrated by citing ten idioms used in the United States. If any of these were to be used in Quebec, for example, the French translation should not be a literal one but should approximate the local phrase or idiom commonly used there. The U.S. version is mentioned first and is followed by the comparable French-Canadian expression.

1. "To murder the King's English" should be translated as "To speak French like a Spanish cow."

2. "Nothing to sneeze at" should become "Nothing to spit on."

3. "As welcome as a bull in a china shop" should become "As welcome as a dog in a bowling alley."

4. "A little birdie told me so" should become "My little finger told it to me."

5. "To be sitting on the fence" should become "To swim between two streams."

6. "I have a hangover" should become "I have a sore hair."

7. "To cry in one's beer" should become "To have the sad wine."

8. "Unable to make head or tail of it" should become "To lose one's Latin."

9. "To make a mountain out of a molehill" should become "To drown in a glass of water."

10. "You can't teach an old dog new tricks" should become "One does not teach an old monkey to make faces."[7]

It need not be an entire phrase that needs rewording, but only one simple word. What the people of one country take for granted as the only correct word or sound might be totally inappropriate to those in another country. Take, for example, the words used for animal sounds. In reality, an animal makes the same noise in every country, but humans interpret the sound differently from country to country. Therefore:

Translating Can Be Beastly

Every dog may have his day, but whether he has his "bow-wow" depends on the country he lives in and the "language" he speaks. The French pup says "oua oua," but his Japanese counterpart barks out "wan wan;" and in Italy the canine chorus is made up of cries of "bau bau." Dogs in Spain say "guau-guau," in Korea "mong-mong," "vovvov" in Norway, and "hav hav" if their dog-house is located in Istanbul.

Animals, it seems, speak in dozens of "foreign languages" just like us people; and just like our human languages, sometimes their sounds are similar and sometimes not at all alike.

Cats say "meow" in America, and their Polish cousins sound pretty much the same when they "miau," as do felines in Holland who "miauw," in Yugoslavia who "mijau," in France who "miaou," and you'd think a Siamese kitten had English lessons when you hear him "miew." But you may need a translator to help you pet a pussycat in Sweden or Indonesia, where "cat-ese" comes out as "jama" and "ngéong," or in Japan, where "nyaw" is what you'll hear.

If you're out for a ride, don't be surprised when your foreign-born mount refuses to "neigh" and tells you instead "hi-hi" (France) or "hii" (Spain). Down on the farm, hens don't "cluck" in most other countries, either. Those three French hens who arrive on the third day of Christmas are more likely to be saying "glouk-glouk." Chickens who completed Spanish III will, of course, run around the barnyard with a "cloc-cloc" here and a "cloc-cloc" there.

Naturally, this onomatopoeic phraseology represents what the animal sounds like to the human listener's ear. Clearly, many of us hear things pretty much the same way; but not all of us do. Cows say "moo" to English-speaking peoples and rather the same thing to the

French and Spanish, although spelled "meuh" and "muu." So do piggies, who "oink" in America and "groink" on the continent, as do ducks, whose French "coin-coin" or Spanish "cuak-cuak" are not much different from our homegrown "quacks."

Sheep and goats, on the other hand, speak more sharply in French and Spanish than they do in English. The soft "aa" sound of "baa" and "maa" becomes the sharper sound of a stretched long "a" in those languages, as "bé bé," "mé mé," and "bee, mee."

One animal who seems to sound alike to most of the world except us is the king of the barnyard. Only American roosters wake the family with a "cock-a-doodle-doo." In other parts of the world, dawn is heralded by "cocorico" (France), "kikiriki" (Spain), "cutcurigu" (Romania), "cuc-cu-cu" (Vietnam), "chicchirichi" (Italy), "kukurikú (Hungary), "kokoriko" (Turkey), or "kykeliky" (Norway).[8]

Obviously, companies that sell pet food and supplies, and those taking the risky approach of featuring animals in promotions, need to take extra precautions when speaking for these animals. If the messages are to be effective, then the firms must be sure that they are communicating in languages that can be understood.

SUMMARY

Faulty translations have caused the most blunders in international business. These translation mistakes have hindered not only marketing efforts and negotiations but many other aspects of business. They are usually due to carelessness, but language subtleties, words with multiple meanings, and difficult-to-translate idioms also cause problems.

Fortunately, translation blunders are some of the easiest to avoid. Methods to avoid these errors are discussed in chapter 9.

6
MANAGEMENT

"Management: the act, manner, or practice of managing, handling, or controlling something." Certainly a dictionary's basic definition of this word helps us understand why so many blunders can occur in this area of business.

An American executive's mishandling of a presentation prepared for a small Caribbean country serves as a simple example of a management blunder. The meeting was held in the Prime Minister's conference room, and the executive began his presentation with "Honorable Mr. Tollis and esteemed members of the cabinet." The Prime Minister interrupted him several times asking him to start over. Eventually, someone advised the bewildered, and then embarrassed businessman, that Mr. Tollis had been deposed six months earlier.

Unfortunately, people sometimes get careless. Thoughtless conversations, however, can prove costly. When in a foreign-speaking country, it is easy to forget that some of the natives may understand many languages. All too often, speakers learn too late that others understand what they are saying. In fact, visitors to the United States often assume no one understands their native tongue and then promptly say something they regret. An Italian businessman, for example, reportedly flew to Los Angeles to talk with a potential American investor. The Italian was picked up at the airport by the driver of the

American investor. Believing that the driver did not understand Italian, the visitor, speaking in Italian, apparently made some very negative remarks about the potential investor to his accompanying business associate. These remarks were reported by the driver, who did indeed understand what was being said, and the business deal collapsed.

There are many facets of management. Consider Renault, which like many firms has tried to use various barter plans but has experienced mixed success. Trading cars for other products can be profitable, but only if the traded products are correctly marketed. In order to sell its cars in South America, Renault agreed to accept coffee beans in payment. The plan seemed safe since coffee beans are easily traded on world commodity markets. Renault's problems began when the company decided to use the beans to produce instant coffee rather than simply sell the coffee beans wholesale. Without carefully checking the credentials of a fast-talking businessman, Renault agreed to build two plants employing his "miracle new process" for the production of instant coffee. Renault later learned that its new associate had earlier run into legal problems with some of his other international business schemes, but not before it discovered that the so-called miracle process failed to work properly and that its new associate had disappeared. Renault lost about $120 million but learned a valuable lesson.

In 1967 Litton Industries signed a contract with the Greek government to develop two regions of Greece economically. The contract was terminated within three years, however, because the firm failed miserably to deliver on its promises. People are still trying to explain why Litton failed. There are several possible reasons that may have contributed to the failure. It seems that the managers at the time greatly underestimated the tasks involved. The managers also tried to use American management techniques and did not involve local experts in the development project. Nor did they realize that their actions offended the Greek population and threatened the local business community that they had basically ignored.

Imperial-Eastman Corporation, a chemical manufacturer, encountered numerous problems in the operations of its various overseas enterprises. In at least one instance, the company experienced unexpected difficulties when it failed to retain its overseas U.S. personnel for a long enough period of time. Before the operation's critical startup period was completely past, the company relieved its U.S. personnel and relied solely on its locally hired staff to continue running the operation. However, as critical problems developed, Imperial-Eastman discovered that the local staff was not sufficiently experienced to handle the difficult problems resulting from the new operation. In other ventures, the company suffered from poor estimates of initial inventory needs that in turn created production delivery disruptions. Losses were incurred when the firm did not allow for delayed delivery and subcontractors failed to deliver on time.

A precarious balance seems to exist between the number of foreign managers and the number of U.S. managers needed for a successful operation. Imperial-Eastman experienced problems by relying too heavily on inexperienced local managers, but General Electric encountered troubles by its placement and retention of U.S. employees in most managerial positions. In some cases, because the U.S. employees were unfamiliar with the local business practices, they unknowingly nullified the firm's ability to compete with local business people.

General Electric encountered more culturally oriented management problems in France. Its French employees were upset when they were ordered to wear GE T-shirts to one function (too American), post English-language posters, and in general behave as if the subsidiary were an extension of America. Eventually, compromises were made on both sides, but morale already had been badly damaged.

The cases cited above are typical of the types of management blunders that have plagued multinational corporations. Management problems are most often caused by cultural differences that outside managers do not understand and by labor practices with which they are unfamiliar.

CULTURAL DIFFERENCES

A Korean firm, Kunja Industrial Co., which owns the Kunja Knitting Mills plant in South Carolina, recently made the news when an American employee innocently "crooked" his index finger while trying to catch the attention of his Korean boss and motion him to come closer. The employee succeeded in getting attention all right. However, he certainly didn't succeed in getting his boss physically or emotionally any closer. In fact, he was almost fired. The American finger-crooking gesture for asking someone to come closer is considered vulgar in Korea.

When dismissing an employee, it is wise to know the proper way to do it. This is a difficult task to perform in familiar territory but it is especially tricky when one is in a foreign country and does not always fully understand the local culture. An American manager stationed in Indonesia reportedly discovered this recently when he tried to fire an oil rig employee. Rather than notifying the employee privately of his dismissal, the manager publicly told the timekeeper to send the man "packing." In Indonesia, this public dismissal was considered an unacceptable loss of face, which offended both the dismissed man and his friends. So, rather than leave quietly, the man grabbed fire axes and ran after the American manager. Reportedly, the American was barely rescued in time. Obviously, it is dangerous to ignore local management practices and customs.

In a related example of employee dismissal, an American company went to a great deal of expense to carefully plan a massive layoff in one of its European subsidiaries. Just before the plan was implemented, however, the firm learned that such layoffs were illegal. Time and money could easily have been saved had managers known of the local labor laws.

Another American manager was sent to Malaysia to close a major deal. While there, he was introduced to someone he thought was named Roger so he proceeded to call him "Rog" several times during the negotiations. Unfortunately, this important potential client was a *rajah,* which is an important Malaysian title of nobility. The American tendency to use first names, and even more familiar abbreviated names, was the cause of a serious error in this case. Rather than showing respect, the American manager appeared disrespectful and insensitive. When the error was discovered, the damage had been done. It is always best to know who you are dealing with in advance and how that person prefers to be addressed.

The acquisition of the Firestone tire company by Japan's Bridgestone did not proceed as smoothly as hoped. In fact, John Nevin, the crusty former chairman of Firestone, admitted that his style appeared abrupt and abrasive at times to the Japanese whose manner is much more subtle. He needed to be less direct and forceful with them, and they had to become more aware of American-style directness. Both sides tried to adjust, but new managers eventually had to be brought in.

Milwaukee-based Manpower chairman, Mitchell Fromstein, reports that Blue Arrow, a British employment firm, took over Manpower in 1987 but put little effort into understanding how the American labor market differed from the British market. Even the company newsletter directed to the American market ignored American interests. American managers began to openly rebel. Eventually, the Americans wound up in control of the combined company.

In Las Vegas, the Japanese owners of the Aladdin and Dunes Hotel casinos reportedly ran into problems when they tried to use Japanese management techniques. Among other things, they tried to make decisions the typical Japanese way – by consensus. The approach works well in Japan for many firms but was considered too slow and cumbersome in the fast-moving casino environment.

In a wave of ethnocentrism the new American owners of a Spanish company changed the firm's previous prestigious Spanish name to that of the U.S. parent, flew the American flag from the company flagpole, and widely announced the sophisticated and superb technology being introduced. The company even suggested that those who had managed the company prior to the takeover by the Americans were incompetent. Then in a special interview with a prominent U.S. business publication, the new management elaborated on its revamping of the entire Spanish company by boasting that its efforts had succeeded in rejuvenating the floundering Spanish operation. Naturally, the article found its way back to the Spanish public and greatly angered the Spanish employees of the company. In fact, the blunder was so serious that it resulted in a general slowdown of work (strikes at that time were officially banned). The Spanish press released an extremely damaging attack, and local authorities made it difficult for the company to conduct business. The result: The newly acquired subsidiary lost a great deal of its previous business.

Poor Personnel Choices

Just as in any domestic employment position, if a firm places an inappropriate person in an international job, the results can prove disastrous. Several companies have blundered by placing culturally insensitive individuals in sensitive management and sales positions overseas. In one case, a firm introduced a technical product into a market relatively free of competition. Believing that market entry would pose no problem, the company did not pay enough attention to the personal characteristics of the person chosen as its European sales manager. This was unfortunate, because the individual chosen disliked the French and made no effort to ingratiate himself or learn their culture or language. His dislike even spilled over to his abrupt treatment of the sales force. A competitor soon came along and was able to take over much of the market and most of the manager's original sales force.

Similarly, an executive from Lucerne, Switzerland, who was negotiating a business venture with a Japanese firm failed to recognize the importance of personal sentiment to the Japanese. He paid the price. The president of the Japanese company sponsored a party in Tokyo and exclaimed, "I will not do business with a man who does not like us!" The Lucerne executive believed he had concealed his dislike for the Japanese during his stay, but the president of the Japanese company had seen through his mask. The Japanese executive, therefore, refused to proceed with the business deal even though the partnership would undoubtedly have proven mutually profitable.

An employee's attitude, however, is not the only variable of importance. A person may be well intended but simply not qualified for the job. Several such cases can be cited. A major U.S. appliance manufacturer, for instance, experiencing difficulties in Spain, sent three troubleshooters there to investigate. The company overlooked one important fact: The individuals could not speak Spanish. After repeated efforts to communicate failed, the Spaniards eventually lost respect for the three specialists. The problems worsened until a Spanish-speaking manager was sent. A similar situation occurred in Germany. An American manager who understood little German was sent to Germany to discuss marketing plans with the local German subsidiary managers. The local managers, however, spoke little English. Both sides tried to understand each other, but neither nationality did very well. Eventually they parted, thinking that they were in agreement. It was later discovered that during the meeting many important points had been overlooked, and the company subsequently lost numerous sales opportunities.

Even though a manager maintains the right attitude and speaks the language, a successful performance is not assured. Raytheon hired Italian-Americans to manage operations in Sicily but found that the strategy was not as effective as hoped. In this case the trouble lay in the origins of the managers. Because their family ties were with the mainland and not Sicily, these men were not trusted or accepted.

An effective expatriate manager must possess special abilities and traits if he or she is to avoid blundering. Among the most important characteristics are:

1. An ability to get along well with people.
2. An awareness of cultural differences.
3. Open-mindedness.
4. Tolerance of foreign cultures.
5. Adaptability to new cultures, ideas, and challenges.
6. An ability to adjust quickly to new conditions.

7. An interest in facts, not blind assumptions.

8. Previous business experience.

9. Previous experience with foreign cultures.

10. An ability to learn foreign languages.

This list is by no means complete. With so many necessary characteristics, it is no wonder that business people sometimes make mistakes.

LABOR RELATIONS

Many non-American companies have experienced difficulties adjusting to U.S. labor practices when they acquire American firms. The Japanese have received the most attention concerning this, but Europeans have also encountered their share of troubles. Britain's Grand Met, for example, angered Pillsbury's minority employees when, as the new owner, it fired several black middle managers (including the head of its affirmative action program). In another case, a European firm lost a talented employee when it purchased a company and expected a female executive to start serving coffee at the board meetings. Finally, a Brazilian executive created major problems for his firm when he treated his secretaries in America as personal servants. Not only did he ask them to do his personal shopping, but he even asked them to mend his clothes.

Because of cultural similarities, a Japanese company doing business in Indonesia consistently hired Bataks, members of an ethnic group with characteristics similar to the Japanese. Other Indonesians, however, resented this hiring practice, viewed it as discriminatory, and forced the company to change its policy.

An American tin mining firm had problems retaining native employees in Bolivia even though it paid the employees more than the local competition did. It seems that the problem concerned the method of payment. The U.S. company paid by the week, but the Bolivians preferred to be paid by the hour. Thus, they could take a few hours off from time to time and not risk the loss of an entire week's wages.

Americans ran into trouble in Iran long before the Iranian revolution. One problem encountered by business people was the widespread belief that foreigners discriminated against Iranians. A U.S. company cemented this belief when it promised local employees that American workers would not be treated preferentially, but then provided better health benefits for the American employees. Verbal promises are taken very seriously in Iran, so the firm's failure to keep its promise was viewed as a major breach of trust and as further evidence that foreigners discriminate against Iranians.

Many companies have faced labor troubles in Western Europe where governments tend to protect employees and often make layoffs difficult. Some of the most sensationalized cases have occurred in France. Shortly after World War II ended, many American companies rushed into France, hired people, and enjoyed the ensuing business boom. However, the good times didn't last forever and more than a few firms made the mistake of trying to reduce employment levels. General Motors, Remington Rand, General Electric, and other firms soon found themselves forced to reverse layoff decisions. Italy has likewise been the scene of many unpleasant labor disputes with American firms. Raytheon's layoff attempts eventually forced it to close its plant in Sicily at a loss of many millions of dollars.

Another U.S. firm experienced a different kind of problem. Having a tradition in the United States of holding picnics where management and workers mingled with ease in a comfortable environment, the firm tried to export its company picnic to Spain. To highlight management's "democratic" beliefs, the U.S. executives even dressed as chefs and served the food. However, the picnic failed to help develop the desired rapport between the U.S. managers and the Spanish workers. In fact, it was a very awkward event, as the lower-level staff clung together and did not want to be served by their superiors. When an executive approached their picnic table, everyone stood up. The company quickly learned that Spanish attitudes of class distinction and social groups make the casual socializing of workers with executives very difficult.

The United Kingdom has been the home for some of the best-known labor problems of American companies. Ford Motor Company, for example, ran into hard times in England because the British managers and laborers felt that the American managers received better treatment and more power. Many employees openly resented this apparent favoritism. Several key British executives even quit. The company lowered the number of Americans there, thereby reducing the problem, but many employees still resented decisions from headquarters. At one point, British newspapers ran such headlines as "Local Ford plants can't even build a bathroom without permission from Detroit." Actually, this was not far from the truth at the time. Now that much more power is delegated to the local managers (who are more likely now to be British), Ford's labor relations are much better.

The Robert Arundel textile machinery plant in Stockport, England, had to close down after managers tried to impose American labor practices. Arundel later admitted that it was a mistake to try to change worker habits, but they had thought that production-line work would go better if the traditional tea breaks were discontinued. Employees thought otherwise. It is usually easier to change management practices than to radically alter local work habits.

SUMMARY

Obviously, management practices that work domestically do not necessarily work overseas. Different cultures require that companies take different approaches. Managers need to understand local business procedures, governmental policies, and labor practices. A minor misunderstanding can easily lead to a major blunder, just as the wrong person on the job can lead to disaster.

7

STRATEGIC MANAGEMENT

Companies have committed a wide variety of strategic mistakes over the years. Many have been related to their choice of how to enter the foreign market. Supply decisions, though, have also caused a surprising number of problems. Some of the strategic errors have involved fairly complex issues. Naturally, all of these blunders were regretted.

ENTRY MODE

A company "going international" has a variety of entry methods available to it. Acquiring an existing firm, starting up a new operation, forming a joint venture with a local company, and signing licensing agreements are some of the most popular modes of entry. Each method offers advantages and disadvantages.

It might seem that the creation of a joint venture, for example, would eliminate all of the problems encountered by a company "going overseas." With the combined expertise and efforts of both local and foreign firms, potential problems or possible blunders would surely be eliminated. However, although certain types of errors are definitely less likely, a multitude of other problems can arise and pose serious threats to the venture's success.

More than a few firms have experienced unexpected problems with joint ventures. One U.S. firm that entered into a joint venture with some South American capitalists did not fully comprehend its initial errors until some five years later. At the time of the company's commitment, its South American partners were in favor with those in the local government. However, the joint venture began to gradually experience various forms of host government harassment and, consequently, profits slowly declined. Investment money, effort, and time were lost by the U.S. partner. What had happened? The U.S. company had failed to analyze the situation thoroughly. Early research should have revealed both the existence of a volatile political scene and the high degree of political involvement in local business practices.

Dow Chemical Company's joint venture in Korea also failed for many reasons, but one important cause was poor communication. Misunderstandings were everywhere. The situation became so bad that Dow Chemical decided to go public with complaints about its partner. This, of course, infuriated the Koreans. In fact, the Koreans felt that they had no choice but to withdraw from the joint venture since anything else would be viewed as a further loss of face.

A company should create a joint venture only after giving the idea careful consideration. Although another firm may be prepared to become a partner, its eagerness does not necessarily assure success. One U.S. manager found this to be especially true. During an inspection of his company's European operations, he met with a number of Belgian pump-manufacturing executives. Because one particular company exhibited a great deal of interest in forming a partnership, a joint enterprise was quickly formed. A Belgian was installed as the president of the new company, and the U.S. firm's manager in Belgium became the vice-president for manufacturing and engineering. However, the combination of friction between these two men and company losses precipitated a crisis. The partnership was dissolved, and the U.S. company bought up all of the Belgian shares at book value. The result: It was many years before the operation became profitable. Undoubtedly, the U.S. firm's unfortunate choice of a partner hindered this venture's success. Partners must be selected with caution, and employee personalities should be considered.

In another case of failure to consider the long-term implications of a business partnership, a bakery products firm contracted to sell its entire line of baked goods through a sole distributor in a developing country. The distributor had really only been interested in carrying a few items and found the tie-in arrangement disagreeable. Therefore, relations between the manufacturer and distributor quickly degenerated to the point where little communication existed between them. A serious decline in sales subsequently occurred. Unfortunately, this information did not reach the manufacturer very quickly, and large quantities of baked goods spoiled.

In 1945, W. R. Grace and Company and a Columbian firm, the Pinturas Colombianas, formed a joint venture. Not long after the creation of this paint-manufacturing partnership, conflict arose partially as a result of the competitive outlets each firm operated independently for the distribution of the paint. Approximately ten years after the venture's formation, Grace and Company was forced to sell its shares to its Colombian partner. Inevitable sources of conflict should not be overlooked during the initial planning stages of a partnership.

Although blunders are often caused by a company's failure to thoroughly investigate potential partners, sometimes a firm's failure to take advantage of a possible joint venture or licensing agreement also results in a suboptimal situation. For instance, shortly after World War II, parts "specifically for use in" equipment manufactured by the Caterpillar Tractor Company began surfacing for sale in various markets. These products had neither been approved nor manufactured by the Caterpillar Company. The firm, however, was unable to establish any legal claims. If the company had initially sought out a local partner, the demand for these similar parts most assuredly would have benefited Caterpillar. As it turned out, the local manufacturers saw no reason to avoid competing with the totally foreign-owned Caterpillar Tractor Company.

Licensing decisions are as difficult to analyze as those decisions involving the creation of a joint venture. Failure to make the correct decision at the right time can result in the loss of substantial long-range business prospects and potential profits. In one case, a U.S. manufacturer not only licensed the manufacture and sale of its products to an English firm, but also granted the firm the exclusive right to sublicense the U.S. expertise to other countries. At the time the decision was made, the company was not interested in expanding overseas. The firm believed that it was best to simply collect the royalties and thus eliminate its need to provide additional investment money. Within a few years, however, worldwide markets for the firm's products developed. Naturally, the company greatly regretted its earlier decision to permit exclusive licensing.

A similar case involved a U.S. pharmaceutical firm that licensed its manufacturing techniques to an Asian company. The Asian company, heavily promoting the products, enjoyed great success. As a result of the licensing terms, however, the Asian partner reaped almost all of the tremendous profits. Having never realized the product's potential, the U.S. company had permitted the licensing. If the U.S. firm had committed to a more direct form of involvement, such as equity participation, it could have earned greater profits. In this instance, the company's failure to carefully study the market and product opportunities eventually resulted in a lost opportunity.

Sometimes the licensee, although pleased to have been granted the license, is not as enthusiastic about the product as the licensor. One U.S. firm discovered this when it granted an exclusive license to a Japanese company. The Japanese company was given the right to manufacture and sell one of the U.S. firm's specialty products for a period of 20 years. Market studies had indicated that the product, which had been extremely successful in the United States, was destined to replace some of the more conventional materials currently in use in Japan. The U.S. firm had carefully studied its potential licensees and had chosen the Japanese company because of its strength of distribution, size, and record of profit performance. However, the Japanese firm, continuing to push the more conventional materials, failed to promote the new product actively. Since the contract included no agreement concerning minimum royalties, the U.S. company earned no income for the first ten years. Having failed to recognize the Japanese company's marketing initiatives and lack of interest, the U.S. firm was forced to accept the fact that it could not enter the market itself until the expiration of the 20-year license.

Many other firms have also suffered because of their lack of foresight. Consider the U.S. company that manufactured military equipment during World War II. Having failed to engage in product modification or to establish service facilities, the company's highly regarded reputation began to diminish when the war ended. To reestablish its prior position, it hurriedly agreed to a licensing arrangement with a European manufacturer. The agreement permitted the exchange and sharing of information, design, and product development. Not long after the commitment had been made, a market for similar products opened up in Europe. However, because of the licensing agreement, the U.S. firm was essentially excluded from any direct participation in the European market. The European licensee reaped the substantial profits and, being exposed to the expertise of the U.S. company, even became the U.S. company's main European competitor.

The natural tendency for any company is to "get in while the going is good." One U.S. firm particularly eager to begin operations in India quickly negotiated terms and completed arrangements with its local partners. Certain required documents, however, such as the industrial license, foreign collaboration agreements, capital issues permit, and import licenses for machinery and equipment, were slow in being issued. Trying to expedite governmental approval of these items, the U.S. firm agreed to accept a lower royalty fee than originally stipulated. Despite all of this extra effort, the project was not greatly expedited, and the lower royalty fee reduced the firm's profit by approximately half a million dollars over the life of the agreement.

Warner-Lambert ran into major problems in its eagerness to sell Trident, Chiclets, and other brands of chewing gum to the Japanese. Because its local wholesalers were not promoting the products to the extent Warner-Lambert desired, the firm decided to change its strategy. The company tried to bypass its wholesalers but quickly realized its mistake. Not only did this move upset the wholesalers, but it also created suspicions among the retailers who often consider companies unreliable if they switch business tactics. To recover, the company asked its sales force to collect the retail sales orders for the wholesalers.

Heinz also experienced difficulties in the Japanese market. Attempting to enter the market quickly, Heinz gained a minority interest in a company called Nichiro Fisheries. Not only did the fishery name imply that all the products were fish-oriented, but the partnership simply was not appropriate. Nichiro Fisheries did not hold enough capital nor did it maintain the broad distribution channels necessary to market Heinz's products adequately.

Failing to consider the values or reliability of a potential partner can also prove disastrous. In some countries, it is normal for a company to take whatever it can from its partner. When both parties expect this, reasonable safeguards can be established. When one company is not aware of this practice, though, blunders can certainly result. For example, a U.S. chemical manufacturer agreed to a partnership after being visited by some overseas managers. The strategy developed involved the export of raw materials by the U.S. firm and the manufacture of products by the foreign company. All of the details were carefully stipulated in the contract, but within six months of the first large shipment of raw materials, the partnership broke up. What had gone wrong? Credit terms had not been met, earnings were disputed, and payments had not been sent. The well-known local partner had gained part of his visibility through his ability to delay or avoid paying his obligations – a common local practice. The U.S. company should have been aware of this custom. It then would have known to require payment in advance (the locally accepted practice) or to establish some other financially safe arrangement. To the local courts, the U.S. firm appeared foolish and deserved the loss. After all, the company had failed to follow sound, normal business practices.

SUPPLY PROBLEMS

Most companies try to save money by purchasing supplies in large quantities. There are, however, logical limits governing this strategy. One example of excessive purchasing occurred in Chile. Until recently, the Chilean government levied high tariffs on automobile imports. Over time, this policy created a large, pent-up demand for cars. In the late 1970s, the government began to radically reduce tariffs and, consequently, demand quickly outstripped supply. By 1981, these tariffs had dropped so low that large numbers of Chileans could afford new autos. Because dealers were unable to fill the vast number of orders, a five-month waiting period for most automobile models was not unusual. Believing that this demand might be unlimited, dealers ordered up to ten times their normal number of cars for 1982 even though the economy began experiencing a recession and the new models were higher-priced. A flooded market resulted. Most of the demand for autos had already been satisfied, and few of the fairly new cars needed to be replaced. Economic uncertainty and higher prices also kept customers away. The result was that inventories grew so high that dealers had no room to store the cars. Many loads (more than a year's supply) were left on board ships lying offshore, incurring high storage costs. The lesson: Optimistic, straight-line projections of sales figures are obviously dangerous. Temporary causes of demand should be analyzed and estimates made to determine the amount of pent-up demand still remaining.

Nigeria, though, probably experienced the largest purchasing blunder. Due to increased oil revenues that resulted from the sharp rise of oil prices in the mid 1970s, Nigeria began to initiate major modernization programs. An economically minded bureaucrat decided to purchase, mostly from other countries, the total amount of cement needed to construct all of the new buildings being planned. Soon the cement began to arrive by the shipload. The dockworkers were unable to unload the cement as fast as it arrived, so the ships were forced to await their turn for unloading. Within weeks, there were so many shiploads of unloaded cement that someone computed the length of time required to unload all of the ships. Even with an expanded dock in Lagos, it was calculated that the 20 million tons of cement could not be fully unloaded for 40 years! Much of the cement had to be dumped overboard, because the cost of delaying the ships until unloading was greater than the cost of reordering the cement.

EverReady, Ltd, of England, encountered supply problems of a different nature. Hoping to introduce its product to the Nigerians, the company chose a strategy that stressed broad market penetration. The EverReady name and battery were heavily promoted, and a large production run was shipped to Lagos. No problems occurred during the unloading, but the firm probably wished that some had. Apparently a defective chemical had been used during the production of the batteries, and those shipped to Lagos were worthless. Unfortunately, someone had forgotten to test them prior to shipment. Although the first batteries appearing on the heavily promoted Nigerian market sold quickly, word soon spread that the product was not dependable. Since no backup supply of good batteries was available, the promotional effort was wasted, and the firm developed a reputation in Nigeria as being an unreliable company that produced poor goods. Later, when normal batteries reached the Nigerian market, consumers avoided them. It took years for EverReady to overcome its initial poor reputation there.

Large department stores often purchase stock from many sources, including foreign countries. It is especially important for the buyers of these goods to be familiar with local foreign customs. They should also be fluent in the required language or procure translation assistance. One overconfident buyer created quite a problem for her Italian firm. Believing that she knew English fairly well, she was sent to Britain to purchase clothing. When she found some appropriate sweaters at Bourne and Hollingsworth, a supplier, she attempted to request "four to five thousand pounds worth." It became quite obvious, however, that there had been a "misunderstanding" when she returned to Italy and the delivery trucks began arriving. They were carrying the *forty-five* thousand pounds worth (approximately $90,000 U.S.) that she had actually ordered.

Often a company is initially successful overseas but later experiences major difficulties. This occurred for one company that located in Africa. The firm began purchasing huge supplies of old, used inner tubes discarded by the U.S. Army during World War II. These inexpensive discards were easily cut to form rubber bands, and soon the company had captured the entire local rubber band market. After making over $1 million on the venture, the owners felt extremely clever and successful until someone pointed out that the supply of old inner tubes had dried up. The war was over, the army had left, and the newer tires of the few vehicles still in use were tubeless. Awash with money and confidence, the managers decided to "go big league" and buy modern equipment. The machinery and supplies, of course, were expensive and difficult to maintain. The company, unskilled at the new process and failing to realize how different the new system would be, was unable to produce rubber bands at affordable prices. The strategy failed, and all of the former profits were lost.

Supply difficulties have hindered a number of companies. Recall an earlier example from chapter 2, where one U.S. pineapple firm was unable to transport its fruit down the river to its processing plant because it had failed to analyze the typical river conditions. Similarly, the Soviet Union built a large, expensive steel mill for India only to discover that the mill had been located in an area with inadequate transportation facilities. The steel mill, intended as a showplace for Soviet propaganda purposes, became an embarrassment instead.

Another firm developed problems when it tried to buy steel plates from Japanese manufacturers. At the root of this blunder was the company's failure to understand the Japanese tendency to say "yes" in order to sound agreeable. By inviting all of the Japanese plate producers to bid, the company felt that it would attain the lowest price. The low bidder offered to sell at such an appealing price that the firm decided to order all of the needed galvanized steel plates from that particular Japanese company. The Japanese firm was first contacted, however, to assure product availability since the quantity required was so large. "Yes," the company responded; it would fill the large order. The U.S. corporation confidently awaited the shipment. Eventually a small, partial shipment arrived containing plates that had obviously been hand-dipped. Since during the normal production process, machines do all of the dipping, the U.S. firm became suspicious. Upon visiting the Japanese plant, its suspicions were confirmed. The plant was quite small and simply could not supply the necessary quantities. Although the Japanese managers knew this would be the case, they did not want to lose face by admitting that their company was so small. They had simply hoped to meet the demand.

COMPLEX PROBLEMS

Although some of the strategic errors committed by multi-national corporations are fairly easy to understand, others are complex and involve several components. The Simmons Company, Ford Motor Company, Raytheon, and General Electric have all experienced complex problems within their foreign operations.

The Simmons Company, a marketer of quality beds, might never have taken the plunge to expand into Japan if it had known the magnitude of the problems it would encounter. With numerous successful overseas ventures under its belt and confident of its product, the Simmons Company set out in the early 1960s to manufacture mattresses in Japan. Four years later, the company was still experiencing substantial losses in Japan. Several complex problems plagued its operation. Although aware of many of the difficulties surrounding the Japanese market, the company had underestimated the degree of complexity present in the Japanese environment.

From the start, Simmons had realized that it would face several obstacles. Not only did most Japanese still sleep on futons (a type of floor mat), but the company also recognized that the complex and unusual Japanese distribution system could be quite confusing. The fact that an oligopolistic group of local manufacturers historically vied for control of the limited market only complicated matters further.

However, because the firm strongly believed in its product and know-how, Simmons Tokyo (later, Simmons Japan) was organized in October 1964. Entry into the market had been timed to coincide with the Tokyo Olympic Games when the demand for beds would sharply rise over a short period of time. Early production progressed smoothly, but problems developed later.

Among the difficulties the company initially encountered was its choice of a sales force. Because of the existence of social class differences and subtle language styles, the salesmen were most effective if they and the client were of the same class. Therefore, the initial eight-man sales force had to be rigorously screened. Even after an appropriate personnel choice, a problem ensued. None of the salesmen had ever slept on a bed. How could they be expected to sincerely endorse Simmons's product?

Simmons also learned that it had priced each its beds by as much as $60 above domestic prices. Even the distribution system proved baffling, since everyday conduct and favors were often intertwined. A customer might engage in business with a supplier to whom he owed a favor regardless of the price difference, and this behavior produced a tangled distribution network with complex relationships. Since no Japanese wished to lose face, Simmons also discovered that trying to operate outside of this established system was quite difficult.

And finally, Simmons made an unfortunate decision regarding advertising media. The company chose print media and concentrated its distribution in the Tokyo area instead of using television, the most effective and penetrating advertising medium in Japan.

Another U.S. firm encountered other types of problems in its efforts to "go international." An electronics firm was approached by a foreign firm interested in creating a joint venture in Asia. Because the product potential appeared so high, the company wished to fully establish the venture before any competition could be enticed into the market. So an agreement was quickly arranged. In its haste, however, the U.S. firm failed to investigate completely such important marketing factors as competitive environment, market maturity, distribution requirements, marketing costs, penetration strategy, promotional programs, and so forth. Nor did the U.S. company carefully evaluate its partner's experience, general know-how, and operational procedures. As a result, problems that should have been considered and resolved during the initial planning stages of the venture were still cropping up years later.

Ford Motor Company has established a very successful record in international business. In fact, it has been the most successful U.S. automotive company to engage in business outside of North America. Even Ford, however, has encountered its share of troubles. In 1973, for instance, after experiencing great success in the Philippines with its Fiera, Ford introduced the vehicle in Thailand. It sold poorly, however. Ford had overestimated its reputation and had incorrectly assumed that Thai consumers would prefer a Ford to other cars. The company had also assumed that the Fiera's low price would attract customers, but it was not prepared to offer the credit terms extended by its competitors. Furthermore, the Fiera frequently experienced breakdowns because vehicles in Thailand were usually loaded two or three times beyond normally designed capacities. By the time a sturdier model was introduced, the Fiera had already earned a reputation for being unreliable.

When Raytheon's local partner withdrew from its Sicilian joint venture due to declining profits, Raytheon was unable to find a replacement partner for its television tube–producing plant. The plant needed modernization, but the needed modifications required substantial capital investment. Thus, Raytheon tried to continue selling out-of-date tubes. Not only were the tubes outdated, but the market was saturated. The company failed to develop any export markets even though sales had dropped significantly in Italy. Losses continued to mount, so the firm fired one-fourth of its employees. The dismissal of Sicilian employees without prior governmental approval and without major payments to those involved, however, was an extremely unacceptable business practice. The result: Local government officials took control of the plant, and Raytheon lost over $25 million.

In a different part of Europe, another large U.S. corporation came very close to committing a similar error. To realize substantial cost savings, the company planned a massive cost reduction program that involved the layoff of a significant number of employees. It was fortunate for the company that prior to the initiation of the program, it learned that layoffs based on these grounds were highly unacceptable in the host country. Since much of the firm's business was with agencies of the host government, this action surely would have produced great unhappiness and the government agencies would have been pressured to place their orders with other suppliers. Sales undoubtedly would have dropped, but even more damaging and far-reaching would have been the company's loss of reputation. Indeed the blunder was avoided, but the company had needlessly allocated time and money to develop a plan that never could have worked. Much inefficiency could have been avoided had the corporation been aware of this local business practice.

General Electric also experienced trouble overseas. The company was initially so optimistic and enthusiastic about some of its foreign ventures that its unrealistic original projections and timetables often led to disappointment. Because of these early letdowns, management tended to be wary of complete ownership or majority interest in its overseas operations. And in some South American projects the company tried too long to maintain the distribution channels it had developed over the years. By doing so, it became particularly vulnerable to the rise of innovative competition during a period of rapidly changing environments, and thus failed to aggressively seek out and adopt new methods of distribution.

ADDITIONAL MISTAKES

Sometimes a company finds that its golden touch is not golden everywhere. The Tengelmann group of West Germany discovered this when it bought an American supermarket chain, the A&P. The firm's normal strategy of offering a limited line of low-cost, store-brand groceries worked well for Tengelmann in Europe. However, its attempts to use this same strategy in the United States failed and resulted in a $75 million loss over a two-year period. As the new chairman, James Wood, admitted, "The mistake we foreigners often make is to judge the U.S. on the basis of what we know about Europe. Americans want a fuller range of products from a supermarket than [do] people on the other side of the water."[9]

Foreign firms often get tripped up in the United States because they fail to develop clear strategies unique to their U.S. operations. Extensions of home strategies often are inappropriate, but foreign-owned firms seem determined to learn this the hard way. The purchase of the A. B. Dick Company by General Electric of Britain is a case in point. Because the British firm did well in the United Kingdom advertising and selling its "modern" office products, it promoted this theme when marketing A. B. Dick products in the United States. The problem? Eighty percent of the A. B. Dick products were not modern, and so the company's strategy was ineffective.

Europeans, of course, are not the only ones who sometimes assume that what works at home will also work abroad. A highly successful American supermarket chain experienced difficulties in its overseas venture. The American company and a renowned Japanese company, Sumitomo Shoji Kaisha, Ltd, formed a supermarket joint venture in Japan. Small Japanese retailers, however, strongly objected to the bond created by these two giants, so Sumitomo Shoji helped set up a dummy company and permitted the U.S. firm to manage it. The U.S. company employed the techniques proven successful in U.S. supermarket management but could not produce profitable financial statements in Japan. After studying the Japanese distribution system, the traditional Japanese ways of doing business, and the characteristics of the Japanese customers, the U.S. management decided that it was necessary to convert the operations to a "Japanese mode." The Japanese customers found the new system acceptable, and the venture began to thrive.

The Parker Pen Company decided to streamline its product line and "globalize" its operations. During the 1980s, it reduced its global product line from 500 styles in about 150 countries to 100 pen styles and decided to use a single international campaign. The concept sounded fine in theory and certainly permitted real production and marketing savings, but it created serious morale problems for Parker's managers. Overseas managers resented the U.S.-mandated plan. Profits sank, management rebelled, and the promotional strategy was eventually discontinued. Parker Pen now lets local managers determine promotional plans.

In another case, a U.S. consumer products firm developed a plan to create a world structure of subsidiaries through the acquisition of similar companies located in both developed and developing countries. Through these subsidiaries, it hoped to form a worldwide market for its products. Therefore, small-

and medium-sized companies in Europe, Latin America, and Japan were purchased within a three-year period. Special efforts were made to add the U.S. products to the existing lines of the acquired companies, since the consumer goods available through these foreign companies were different from those in the parent's line. However, the U.S. company ran into several problems using this strategy. Not only had it failed to consider the tastes of its potential customers, but in most cases the U.S. products did not even meet foreign requirements. Furthermore, the marketing, advertising, and promotional techniques that had produced such a long record of company success in the United States were not appropriate for the foreign environments. Due to the lack of supermarkets and retail chain outlets, lower standards of living, limited TV advertising exposure, and lower levels of literacy, the U.S. techniques proved ineffective in these new markets.

Many cases can be cited to underscore the importance of conducting a thorough preliminary market study. Consider, for example, the U.S. company that discovered that its failure to understand its Japanese partner's distribution network greatly hindered the venture's success. Hoping to achieve optimum market penetration for its product, which was relatively new to the Japanese, the U.S. firm selected the best distribution networks of its Japanese partner and set up a single-level system of wholesalers. Even though the product sold well through the selected distribution channels, market penetration fell short of expectation because the product did not receive the needed national coverage. The original decision to use the partner's best distribution networks appeared wise, but the firm both failed to fully realize how numerous and diffuse the Japanese retail outlet networks can be and overestimated the effectiveness of its planned network.

Distribution problems do not only occur within the Japanese system. Having received encouraging results from a preliminary market study, a major U.S. manufacturer of mixed feed for poultry decided to establish a market in Spain. Although local business people advised the firm against forming a subsidiary that was foreign-owned, the company went ahead with its plans. A factory was built, a technical staff was brought in, and operations were set up. However, once production began, the firm discovered that it could not sell its products. Why? The Spanish poultry growers and feed producers comprised a closely knit group, and newcomers were not welcome. To overcome this obstacle, the firm bought a series of chicken farms to support its feed production. To its dismay, the company discovered that no one would buy its chickens either. Had the company heeded the local advice and understood the local business practices, these difficulties could have been avoided.

Many other companies have suffered similar setbacks. For instance, one American cosmetics manufacturer experienced difficulties when it tried to sell its products in France solely through a chain store. By utilizing this method, the firm felt it could achieve maximum market exposure and still hold down marketing and distribution costs. In some countries, this system might have worked. In France, however, *parfumeurs* (small local retailers specializing in cosmetics) are traditionally considered the opinion makers, and most manufacturers grant exclusive franchise to two or three local perfumers. Word-of-mouth promotion is vital, and the public relies heavily on the opinions of these perfumers. When it bypassed them, the American company angered the perfumers to the point of discrediting the American product and damaging the manufacturer's reputation in France.

Conversely, foreign firms have encountered problems in developing viable strategies for the U.S. market. Asuag A6, a Swiss watchmaker, realized this need for a viable strategy too late. The firm needed to acquire technology and decided to do so by purchasing a dozen different U.S. firms. Although some of the companies proved useful to the watchmaker, they did not seem to fit together well. Many firms were not even compatible with others in the acquisition package. Trying to coordinate them only made matters worse. All twelve were eventually sold – at a loss of over $25 million dollars.

Fujitec, a Japanese elevator manufacturer, came to the Unted States with high aspirations – too high as it turned out. Rather than concentrate on one geographical area, the firm simultaneously sought out large projects all over the country. However, it apparently failed to recognize the regional preferences of U.S. consumers and tried to approach the market as if none existed. As a consequence, the company did not consider important cultural subtleties and lost money. Japan may be a fairly homogeneous market, but the U.S. market is not. Few companies have the ability to enter all regions at the same time. Most find that they need business experience in one or two regions of the United States before they can attempt a national campaign.

A clear, consistent strategy is required if a company is to succeed in the international marketplace. Companies have experienced a great many difficulties as a result of poor strategy decisions. As an illustration, consider the aerospace division of Ling-Temco-Vought (LTV), which tried to create a mechanical substitute for the water buffalo. Because the company's research and development facilities were located in the United States, the firm developed the machine in the United States. Unfortunately, this was not a wise decision. The machines produced by the company were eventually exposed to the unique Asian weather conditions and experienced many unanticipated problems.

Host governmental approval is an another extremely important variable involved in the determination of a company's overseas success. Massey-Ferguson learned this when it reportedly experienced some difficulties after entering into a 51 percent ownership venture in Turkey to produce tractors. A large-scale plan was developed that permitted an initial annual production capacity of 50,000 engines and called for the later addition of a second facility that would produce another 30,000 tractors a year. The company's high hopes were never realized. Massey-Ferguson reportedly failed to thoroughly investigate the economic and political scene in Turkey and the stability of the government. To assure its market success, the company needed strong governmental backing. This support never fully materialized (a result that some claim could have been predicted), and the venture was formally terminated in 1970.[10]

The U.S. lock manufacturer, Yale and Towne, can attest to the desirability of gaining not only local governmental support but also the acceptance of local competitors. In the 1960s, in order to gain entry into the Japanese market, Yale and Towne planned to form a joint venture with Copal Co., Ltd, a local Japanese camera shutter manufacturer. The plans were quite ambitious and included a projected annual production target of 600,000 units, or 20 percent of the Japanese market. Local manufacturers, threatened by these plans, petitioned the Japanese Ministry of International Trade and Industry requesting that the Ministry not allow this investment. Not surprisingly, Yale and Towne experienced a delay in the processing of its application. By April 1965, the local lock industry had been included in a list of industries that fell under the Law for Acceleration of Modernization of Small Enterprise (a section of the 1950 Foreign Investment Law). The industry thereby gained special protection and development incentives from the government. Eventually the Yale and Towne application was rejected. Had the company initially shown more discretion, the local manufacturers may have accepted the new competition without pursuing governmental protection.

An unfortunate decision made by Gillette nearly cost the company the razor blade market. The firm had developed a superior stainless steel blade, but because the new blade was so outstanding and would require fewer replacements, the company preferred not to market it. So Gillette sold the technology to a British garden tool manufacturer, Wilkinson. Because Gillette had assumed that Wilkinson would only use the new technology in the production of its garden tools, it failed to restrict Wilkinson from competing in the razor blade market. However, Wilkinson Sword Blades were promptly introduced in both the United States and Great Britain and sold as fast as they could be produced. Gillette's superior marketing skills and experience in the razor blade market enabled it to eventually recover, but the challenge was unwelcome and expensive.

SUMMARY

False assumptions frequently cause expensive blunders in strategy. One of the most common assumptions is that conditions that exist at home also exist abroad. Another frequently assumed idea is that what works well at home will also work well overseas. It should be abundantly clear that these are two of the most dangerous assumptions that managers can make. Few things are the same everywhere, and almost no strategy works well globally.

Strategic blunders are generally not as entertaining to read about as are some of the other multinational mistakes, but they are usually more critical to the firm and thus more important to avoid. Although some mistakes can be quickly corrected, logistical problems can be very difficult to overcome. A few strategic blunders have even resulted in millions of lost dollars. There are no simple shortcuts to avoid strategic errors. The development of a strategy requires care and attention to detail.

8

OTHER AREAS OF
INTERNATIONAL BUSINESS

The previous chapters have contained numerous examples of blunders made in the areas of production, translation, name choices, marketing, management, and strategy. These types of blunders are frequently committed and often quite visible. Once made, these mistakes can be rather difficult to conceal. Blunders occurring in the other areas of business – such as law, finance, and market research – are either less frequently committed or easier to hide. They certainly are not reported as often, but they can be just as costly or critical to the success of the business venture.

LAW

The legal details involved in any transaction certainly can seem confusing and boring. However, a lack of awareness or understanding of these technicalities can prove to be disastrous as illustrated by the plight of an American transacting business in Saudi Arabia. A Californian reportedly found himself trapped in Saudi Arabia as a result of a dispute he was having with his Saudi partner. The Saudi, an associate in a janitorial supplies venture, sponsored his Californian partner's entry into Saudi Arabia early in 1982, but refused to sponsor the man's departure unless he was paid the $100,000 he claimed was owed to him. Under Saudi law, a foreigner cannot leave the country without the endorsement of the person who sponsored his entry. The American settled by paying $55,000. "It was the only way I could get out," he said. The problem might have been avoided had he insisted in advance on a written agreement with the Saudi.

An American firm discovered the value of using clear and concise contractual language when one of its West African contract clauses cost the company about $100,000. The troublesome clause read, "The monies paid by the Ministry to the Consultant shall constitute full payment to the Consultant including all local income taxes on the Consultant." The firm understood this to mean that payments were tax-free. The government ruled otherwise. And since another clause in the contract said that disagreements were to be settled by the local government, the firm naturally lost.

A Columbus, Ohio company committed a "minor" error in filling out a form in Brazil. Unfortunately, this mistake resulted in the firm being unable to withdraw $200,000 in profits it eventually earned there. What was the so-called minor error? Someone had failed to place a check in a box on the document that would have allowed the company to withdraw profits at a reasonable rate.

AT&T experienced troubles in Thailand in 1989 trying to obtain a major phone equipment contract. After a great deal of effort, AT&T submitted a proposal that was promptly rejected. Apparently, Thailand had specified that a ten-year warranty was required, but the AT&T lawyers working out of the U.S. proposed a five-year warranty. The company's employees and contacts in Thailand understood the requirement, but the contract had been drawn up by lawyers thousands of miles away. In fact, AT&T has had such little hands-on overseas experience that as late as 1989, when an emergency meeting was called in Italy, several of its U.S.-based "international" managers had to reveal that they did not even own passports.

Most countries have now established regulations for monitoring advertising. As many companies can avow, failure to follow these guidelines almost always results in a legal dispute. Singapore's airline can attest to this. The company placed advertisements in local Norwegian magazines featuring a photo of a girl's face on a pillow. The message essentially said, "Bring me a pillow and brandy for a tired father." The Norwegians were upset with the ad, and eventually the promotion was ruled misleading and sexually discriminatory.

Similarly, the use of a commercial featuring a bikini-clad woman created difficulties for Goodyear. The advertisement apparently was shown in several countries where such skimpy attire was not locally permitted. The company, forced to alter the commercial, replaced the young model with fully dressed people having a good time. The message, "Get where the fun is," remained unchanged, but the revised commercial was considered more acceptable and effective.

Goodyear Tire also experienced legal problems with an advertisement it tried to export to Germany. The ad, successfully used in the United States, highlighted the strength of Goodyear's tire cord by showing that it could break a steel chain. Goodyear discovered, however, that in Germany it was illegal to imply that another product was inferior. Because Goodyear's promotion was interpreted to be disparaging to the German steel chain manufacturers, the government halted the promotional campaign.

Claridge cigarettes advertised its product in Australia using a campaign that featured Robin Hood and Friar Tuck. Australians, believing that their children might find the ad appealing, felt that the orientation was inappropriate and forced Claridge to alter its advertisements.

Ford experienced a similar problem with one of its ads distributed in Norway. The advertisement featured children talking to a car salesman with the caption, "Is it true that there is a waiting period for Fords?" Local groups complained that it was improper to use the children in the promotion because they were directly connected to neither the product nor the targeted consumer. While such usage could easily be considered harmless and enjoyable by many, a firm must consider potential legal expenses should it find itself defending its ads.

A novel twist occurred in France where Philip Morris, Inc. and the R. J. Reynolds Tobacco Co. were enjoying much financial success. The companies, in fact, were so successful that a local company, SEITA, tried to sell its cigarettes as if they, too, were foreign imports. Their packages bore the name News and were printed totally in English. Not even the well-known French name of the parent company was listed. French law, however, prohibited this omission, and so, in at least this one case, it was the local company that experienced legal difficulties in its effort to thwart foreign competition.

The complexities of foreign investment laws have also been frequent sources of problems. The 3M Company, for example, submitted an application to the Japanese government to establish a joint venture with 15 firms of the Sumitomo industrial group. The company's failure to consider all of the applicable Japanese investment laws delayed the governmental approval required. By the time the approval was obtained – four years later – domestic manufacturers such as Sony and Tokyo Denki Kagaka had succeeded in streamlining the production of magnetic tape products and, unfortunately, Sumitomo-3M's share of the market was held to a very small percentage of the total Japanese market.

False assumptions regarding the level of host government support have led to many problems. Massy-Ferguson, for example, believed it had won Turkish support to establish a tractor-producing plant. The company heavily relied on that support to help with sales. Unfortunately, the support never materialized and the venture eventually died.

Sometimes companies win governmental support when perhaps they should not. For example, it is possible at times to gain legal approval to do (or not do) things that should not (or should) be done. This legal support offers a business protection, but it can prove to be temporary or controversial. Several firms have found all too suddenly that, as times change, the definition of what is acceptable can change.

Consider a company in Spain that obtained permission from the Spanish government to use badly outdated technology that polluted the atmosphere. A sudden change in weather created a dangerous health situation, however. Several people died, the local population rioted, the government withdrew its approval, and the company paid the price for hiding behind the legal protection of the government.

Several U.S. firms have encountered legal problems either at home or abroad because they were affiliated in some way with overseas business operations that "traded with the enemy." U.S. law sometimes forbids American firms to sell certain products to certain countries. Special problems can arise when overseas joint ventures or even licensed firms start trading with these outlawed countries. If the U.S. parent or partner company does not restrict business activity, the U.S. government takes legal action. But, if the U.S. parent or partner discontinues the business overseas, the host government may take legal action of its own. Just because the U.S. government restricts business activities in a country does not mean that all countries curtail business operations there. This can be an awkward, catch-22-type situation – one that is best avoided by anticipating the potential problem and clarifying everything before formalizing any joint venture or signing any agreement.

For example, Fruehauf, a U.S. truck manufacturer, sold truck bodies to a French firm through its French subsidiary. The French firm then finished the trucks and sold them to the People's Republic of China. The U.S. government took action against Fruehauf for selling trucks to China, then an outlawed destination. Consequently, this U.S. behavior caused the French government to seize control of Fruehauf's French subsidiary. France believed that Fruehauf had to honor its contracts – even if that meant selling parts that eventually ended up in China, an acceptable destination to the French. Not only did Fruehauf lose money, but the company became the unwanted center of a highly charged, public debate in France concerning the role of America and its firms in France. At that point, it was clearly a no-win situation that would take years to overcome.

It is absolutely critical to remember that what is legal in one country may not be legal in another. This important lesson applies to many aspects of business, including patent protection of industrial property rights. Many firms have falsely assumed that more protection existed in a foreign country than actually did. If companies are not careful, highly valued trade secrets can be lost with no legal recourse.

Companies may experience troubles by being unaware of a country's regulations and preferences concerning products and packages. The wording on a package or label may create difficulties. Countries expect foreign marketers to adhere to rules, and their failure to do so may prove costly. Coca-Cola, for instance, aroused the anger of the Italians when it printed the mandatory list of ingredients on its bottle cap. Local courts ruled that because the cap was easily tossed away, it did not serve as an acceptable location for this list. Coca-Cola, of course, quickly modified its package and listed the ingredients on the bottles themselves, but the incident was not without its costs.

Many companies have encountered legal problems trying to sell various diet foods because, in several countries, a product name containing the word *diet* can only be sold in pharmacies. Thus, these lighter-in-calories products can now be found on store shelves in some countries with "Lite" used in their names.

In Australia, the manufacturer of Aim toothpaste was taken to court by one of its competitors because of an Australian law that prohibits the sale of competitive products in similar packages. A very strict interpretation and enforcement of this law forced Unilever to change its Aim package even though it had spent $5 million promoting the toothpaste. The error was costly, but it was correctable with the appropriate alterations.[11]

fiNANCE

Small overseas firms are sometimes so impressed with the size and growth of U.S. markets that they forget about the possible risk of a U.S. economic downturn. The U.S. economy may be comparatively wealthy to many people, but it still experiences recessions that the investing firms need to take into consideration. Many foreign-owned firms in the United States have reportedly sunk because they failed to plan for worst-case scenarios.

Since most foreign investors in the United States do not have their stock listed on U.S. markets, they seldom make an acquisition through stock swaps. This means that they are usually forced to borrow money. If the timing is poor or if they do not prepare for market downturns, they can be squeezed unexpectedly. For example, Agache-Willot (a French chain of discount stores) purchased Korvettes, another chain, but was not prepared to invest another $28 million when a subsequent recession was experienced. By the time the firm finally agreed to infuse the additional needed capital, it was really too late. Korvettes went bankrupt a year later.

American firms have also fallen into the temptation of having a very high debt-to-equity ratio. This highly leveraged position works well when times are good, but it is risky and can lead to disasters in bad times. The USM subsidiary in Portugal reportedly became unnecessarily leveraged and then needed the parent company's help to insure its survival. Many others have found themselves in this same situation. In England, the American term *highly leveraged* is nonsensical. Rather, they use the phrase *highly geared*. These different wordings have confused people on both sides of the Atlantic.

An American auto manufacturer in Europe encountered problems of a different nature. The company reportedly failed to consider long-run profit margins. As a result, its Spanish division began experiencing a profit squeeze. The managers tried to cut costs by changing labor workloads, sales commissions, and even production schedules – all to no avail. In fact, labor resisted and costs actually increased.

Misinterpretations can sometimes cause major financial losses. One company, for example, decided to spend $2 million for a Brazilian plant it seems was not needed. The company's decision to invest the money was based upon an incorrect interpretation of data. The reported sales figures (stated in Brazilian *cruzeiros*) appeared very promising, but they had not been adjusted to account for high inflation. Only the number of *cruzeiros* had grown, not the number of products sold. It is often more prudent to evaluate sales levels employing physical measures (such as weight, volume, number of units, etc.) rather than financial ones. Then inflation and currency value fluctuations are less likely to cause such errors.

MARKET RESEARCH

One of the worst errors a company can make is failing to determine if a market exists for its products or services prior to market entry. Unfortunately, many firms have fallen prey to this mistake and blindly assumed that their products would be desired. At times, they have been correct (perhaps "lucky" might be more appropriate). Other times, however, they have not been so fortunate. Often the market simply was not as promising as anticipated. Several firms have discovered only after initial entry attempts that no market ever existed. Sound and thorough market research would have revealed these and other avoidable problems companies have encountered in international business.

Insufficient Market

Companies exporting food products seem to have been especially prone to experiencing difficulty in foreign markets. An American manufacturer of cornflakes, for example, tried to introduce its product in Japan but failed miserably. Since the Japanese were not interested in the general concept of breakfast cereals, how could the manufacturer expect them to purchase cornflakes?

A well-known U.S. soft drink company predicted the existence of a large Indonesian market for its product, but the prediction was based on a faulty market research study. The study was conducted in large Indonesian cities and the results were projected to be representative of the entire population. Unfortunately, major differences existed between rural and urban areas of Indonesia. During the study, the cities housed many foreign visitors who purchased the soft drink. When the company concluded that a major market existed, it set up large bottling and distribution facilities but only realized limited sales to city tourists. In conducting market research tests, it is important to determine who is purchasing the product and how representative they are of the entire population.

After learning that ketchup was not available in Japan, a U.S. company is reported to have shipped the Japanese a large quantity of its popular brand-name ketchup. Unfortunately, the firm did not first determine why ketchup was not already marketed in Japan. The large, affluent Japanese market was so tempting that the company feared that any delay would permit its competition to spot the "opportunity" and capture the market. A market test would have revealed the reason behind the lack of availability of ketchup; soy sauce was the preferred condiment there. The company involved, however, was able to purchase Japanese soy sauce for profitable resale in the United States (a possible variation of the old saying, "If you can't beat'em, join'em").

Kentucky Fried Chicken reportedly found itself in a similar situation when it attempted to enter the Brazilian market. Hoping to eventually open 100 stores, the company began operations in São Paulo. Sales, though, were unexpectedly low. Why? The firm had not thoroughly researched the possible competition. A local variety of low-priced charcoal-broiled chicken was available on almost every corner of the city. Because the locals considered this chicken tastier than the Colonel's recipe, Kentucky Fried Chicken hastily revised its plans and began offering hamburgers, Mexican tacos, and enchiladas. The company's troubles were not over, however, for these food products were practically unknown in Brazil and met with little customer interest.

Unilever, likewise, was forced to temporarily withdraw from one of its foreign markets when it learned the hard way that the French were not interested in frozen foods. Happily, the company was able to reenter the market at a later date by offering products more appealing to the French.

CPC International met some resistance when it first tried to sell its dry Knorr soups in the United States. The company had test-marketed the product by serving passersby a small portion of its already prepared warm soup. After the taste test, the individuals were questioned about buying the product. The research revealed U.S. interest, but sales were very low once the packages were placed on grocery store shelves. Further investigation uncovered that the market tests had not taken into account the American tendency to avoid dry soups. During the testing, those individuals interviewed were unaware that they were tasting a dried soup. Finding the taste quite acceptable, the interviewees indicated they would be willing to buy the product. Had they known that the soup was sold in a dry form and that the preparation required 15–20 minutes of occasional stirring, they would have shown less interest in the product. In this particular case, the soup's method of preparation was extremely important to the consumer, and the company's failure to test for this unique product difference resulted in an unpredicted sluggish market.

Clever marketers often analyze product differences and try to use them to the company's advantage. Based on a research study conducted in the United States, one American firm introduced a new cake mix in England. Believing that the

home baker would enjoy feeling as if he or she were participating in the preparation of the cake mix, the U.S. marketers
devised the scheme to "add an egg." Thinking they had
developed a universal approach, they tried to sell the mix in
England. The mix failed, though; Britons simply do not like
fancy American cakes no matter how they are prepared. They
prefer tough and spongy cakes suitable for accompanying their
afternoon tea.

Numerous companies have also experienced difficulties
when trying to market certain "tasty" products. Tastes desirable to some are often unacceptable to others. Occasionally, a
flavor can be successfully modified, but many times it is just
totally inappropriate. Warner encountered difficulties when it
tried to sell a cinnamon-flavored FRESHEN-UP gum in
Chile. Because the gum's taste was unacceptable there, the
product fared poorly in the marketplace. Coca-Cola also tried
to market a product in Chile with little success. When the
company attempted to introduce a new grape-flavored drink,
it soon discovered that the Chileans were not interested.
Apparently, the Chileans prefer wine as their grape drink.
These examples exemplify why market research can be so
important.

Chase and Sanborn likewise met resistance when it tried to
introduce its instant coffee in France. In the French home, the
consumption of coffee plays a more significant role than in the
English home. Since the preparation of "real" coffee is a ritual
in the life of the French consumer, he or she will generally
reject instant coffee because of its impromptu characteristics.

A poorly located sales outlet can also contribute to an
insufficient market. A classic example involves one of the
oldest U.S. fast-food companies. This firm, having gained a
great deal of domestic experience, decided to open overseas
outlets. Sophisticated techniques were employed by the man-

agement, and the possible location sites were narrowed down to three addresses in Hamburg, Germany. Careful "traffic counts" were undertaken to determine the best location, and the most frequently passed site was then purchased. A store was built, but sales were surprisingly slow. Was the traffic count in error? No. In this case, while it was true that great numbers of people were passing by the location, hamburgers were not foremost on their minds — they went by the hamburger site only because a major bordello was located next door.

McDonald's also chose an inappropriate location when it first expanded into Europe. The company opened an outlet in a suburb of Amsterdam but soon learned that to attract adequate local traffic, the store should have been downtown. Once the company moved into town, sales immediately improved.

Of course, food companies are not the only firms that have had trouble selling products in foreign markets. The Cummins Engine Company of Indiana tried to introduce its diesel engines in Europe. Sales were sluggish because the major European truck manufacturers also produced their own engines. Cummins was not accustomed to this type of integrated system. Although Cummins denies the report that it had been unaware of the extensive integration before it entered the market, the company does concede that the market was more competitive than expected.

A well-known franchised health club based in New York quickly discovered that what sells in America may not sell overseas. Building on its previous success, the firm decided to open a club in Singapore but soon learned that the club did not appeal to the local population. The small expatriate community was delighted with the club, but its numbers were too small to make the club a profitable venture.

Another company tried to market an aerosol spray furniture polish in one of the less developed countries. Analysis of the local average income levels suggested that the surrounding population could afford the product. This type of data, though, can be misleading when most of the wealth is concentrated and owned by a few. Therefore, average income levels can erroneously indicate that many people in a population can afford a product. In this particular case, only the few individuals who enjoyed the highest incomes could afford the "luxury" of an aerosol spray furniture polish. Even they, however, were not very interested in the product; they did not believe that such labor-saving devices were needed for their servants.

Sometimes the relevant factor determining a product's success involves the technological advancement of the potential customer. A sophisticated product may elicit interest during market testing, but it may fail in the marketplace because it receives a predictably erroneous reputation of undependability. Companies have discovered this fact all too frequently. For example, one company manufactured a product far superior to any similar product being used in a particular African nation. Since market tests indicated strong consumer interest, the firm introduced the product. Shortly thereafter, word spread among the locals that the product was not reliable. This was not true, however. The product malfunctioned because the new owners did not understand its maintenance requirements. They refused to oil it even though they were instructed to do so. Because this type of maintenance was atypical of their lifestyle, they soon returned to their earlier, more primitive tools that required no special care. In effect, no market existed for these advanced products.

In some cases, it becomes necessary for a firm to develop a totally new product, one that is completely stripped of frills or complex features. General Motors successfully used this process during the development of its Basic Transportation Vehicle. Singer, too, profited from its introduction of a basic hand-powered sewing machine.

Although the United States consists of 50 states, the country is usually considered one market despite subtle cultural differences that exist among the states. Neighboring districts in other parts of the world, however, often represent vastly different cultures even though they may be as geographically close as neighboring states. This concept is hard for many American managers to fully understand. The Sunbeam Company, for example, assumed that since West Germans consumed substantial amounts of toast, the Italians would also. To the company's misfortune, it soon discovered that this did not prove to be the case. The firm encountered additional problems in Italy when it tried to introduce an electric shaver for women. Although sales had been fairly strong in some parts of Europe, they remained poor in Italy. Apparently Italian women preferred to have unshaven legs.

People speaking similar languages do not necessarily represent totally similar cultures, either. One American company, assuming that a similar language must indicate similar tastes, tried to sell a U.S. after-shave lotion in England. An expensive advertising campaign was launched but failed. Why? The average British male saw no functional value in the use of after-shave lotion and even believed the use of scents to be effeminate.

In a similar case where a lack of demand has thwarted marketing efforts, numerous governments have tried to send aid to developing countries. Sometimes, however, their well-intended gifts have been of little use. At one time, for example, great quantities of milk powder were distributed in South

America. Claiming that the milk made them ill, the natives used it instead to whitewash their houses. Research revealed that the natives were indeed correct. An enzyme necessary for the breakdown of milk is retained by North Americans and Europeans throughout their lives. Many South Americans, on the other hand, retain the enzyme only while of nursing age. Therefore, the older children and adults were unable to digest the milk. No demand for this product existed even though it was free.

At the end of World War II, the U.S. government shipped a load of corn to Bulgaria to help feed the starving people there. However, because the Bulgarians considered corn to be a food fit only for hogs, the corn sat untouched. The Communist party even used this incident to disseminate propaganda proclaiming that the capitalistic United States had sent pig's food to needy people.

Inadequate Feasibility Studies

It should now be obvious that a firm needs to conduct research to determine if an adequate market for its products exists. This research must be performed carefully since an inadequate feasibility study may prove more disastrous for the company than none at all.

For instance, one company that chose to cut costs and save time opted to use a feasibility study that a competitor had conducted earlier. At the time the study was originally undertaken, the investment was regarded favorably by the Asian government and the opportunity seemed encouraging. However, the political atmosphere changed during the time that had elapsed since the study. As a result, the firm built its plant but immediately experienced difficulties. The company's use of an outdated feasibility study caused it to overestimate positive results and underestimate probable problems.

Many firms have created headaches for themselves by acting before sufficient data has been gathered. Consider, for example, a well-known U.S. manufacturer of nondurable consumer goods that formed a partnership with a local Japanese company. The Japanese firm supplied encouraging data so, after a one-week investigation by the assistant to the president, the U.S. manufacturer quickly agreed to the arrangement. Not too surprisingly, the venture fell short of expectations. Even with a complete change of top management, the investment stagnated. The company's hasty entry decision had been based upon an inadequate market analysis and the belief that the market would welcome the entry of prestigious U.S. brands. The firm had assumed that it could easily win the confidence of the marketplace and take over a sizable percentage of it.

After a research team verified the existence of an adequate market, one Swiss pharmaceutical firm built an $8 million manufacturing plant in Southeast Asia. The researchers, though, had overlooked an extremely important feature of the market – the local black market that was controlled by government officials. Because of this added competition, the firm experienced lower earnings than expected and found itself with excess production capacity.

Sometimes what appears to be a thorough feasibility study simply is not. After conducting what it believed was an intensive study, one firm discovered that a number of factors that should have been considered prior to its entrance abroad had been overlooked. Initial research confirmed the desirability of erecting an iron and steel mill, but the mill was forced to close its doors within one year. All equipment was removed and the building was stripped. Those involved in the feasibility study had correctly determined the availability of labor. They had failed, however, to report that the country under consideration was one in which private ownership was inconsistent with the policies of social reform supported by the government. Almost all manufacturing was publicly owned and operated. The laborers, many of whom had been exploited on the farms they had left, were encouraged to believe in "capitalistic exploitation." Consequently, they constantly demanded higher wages and increased benefits. Labor unrest, low output, and poor quality resulted. The feasibility study should have revealed the existence of this popular "public ownership" ideology. Moreover, since another firm had failed earlier in a similar investment for similar reasons, the investors should have been tipped off that a recurrence of the problem was likely.

As a final example, consider the experience of the Rheem company in the Italian market. The firm's initial strategy of buying raw materials from a local firm, ISI, also included selling the finished product, welded pipe, locally. The plan was put into operation, but Rheem soon learned that not only did ISI produce the same welded pipe, it also maintained insider contracts with the major buyer of the pipe – the government. Because Rheem was buying its raw material from ISI, it was unable to undercut ISI's price and, as a foreign-owned firm, it was not able to secure Italian government contracts. Unfortunately, it had not developed any export plans. Thorough research should have uncovered these problems and forced Rheem to consider alternative plans.

As evidenced, a firm's reliance on outdated or incomplete feasibility studies can cause it to blunder. Improperly conducted studies can also create difficulties. This is easily illustrated by a classic story involving the market research conducted some years ago by *Reader's Digest*. The researchers concluded from their findings that more spaghetti was consumed by West Germans and French than by Italians. Further analysis revealed that this false finding surfaced as a result of the questions asked. The survey questions dealt with the purchases of branded and packaged spaghetti. Many Italians, however, buy spaghetti in bulk. By qualifying the way in which the product was purchased, the researchers arrived at a false conclusion about spaghetti consumption. To conduct sound market research, one must pay strict attention to both method and content.

SUMMARY

This chapter has focused on the importance of paying attention to detail. Seemingly minor points of law can create major problems for companies. Financial strategies, market research, and feasibility studies must all be undertaken and conducted with great care. In fact, the significance of meticulous research cannot be stressed enough.

9
LESSONS LEARNED

As discussed in the previous chapters, international businesses can indeed encounter a variety of unexpected developments. Occasionally, some of these surprises benefit the companies involved. Unfortunately, in numerous other instances, the surprises prove to be undesirable and often costly. Many of the troubles encountered by firms in the past actually could have been avoided.

Venturing overseas can be extremely tricky. A company may employ sophisticated management techniques but still blunder if any one detail is overlooked. Even failing to ask the right question can cause a blunder. Unfortunately, there are hundreds of reported cases of companies blundering overseas. These errors are indeed regrettable, but we can learn from them. There is no need to repeat the mistakes others have made.

ADAPTATION

Numerous headaches have resulted when firms have failed to correctly adapt their products or packages to local environments. Sometimes it is only the color of the package that needs to be altered to enhance a product's sales. Since color preferences and symbols vary from country to country, it is wise to seek local advice as the native population is generally aware of so-called bad colors.

A lesser-known variable worthy of consideration is content number. Packages that prominently display a specific number or quantity increase the risk of consumer avoidance. Since many people believe in lucky and unlucky numbers, even the number of products pictured on a label can prove troublesome.

Sometimes it is neither the number displayed on the package nor the color that creates a problem, but rather the picture on the label. In many other instances, the product itself requires alteration. Food, beverages, and tobacco products often need to be modified in order to accommodate the tastes of local consumers. Cigarette manufacturers learned long ago that American brands sell well overseas – if the tobacco is carefully blended to suit local preferences. Products that are not modified to meet local needs face a high risk of failing in the marketplace.

Sometimes the company or product name may require modification. A domestically successful name may be inappropriate or ineffective in a foreign market. Names have created many a humorous, obscene, offensive, or unexpected situation.

NATIONALISM

Many avoidable problems have occurred because managers have been insensitive to the nationalistic feelings of the natives of the host country. It is usually best for companies to maintain low profiles in overseas ventures. There is seldom any need for a firm to try to turn an overseas manufacturing plant into an exact duplicate of its home plant. Companies that have tried to do this have often met stiff resistance from both employees and local customers.

Foreign manufacturers in the United States learned this lesson long ago. Many American laborers are now working for foreign-owned firms but remain unaware of their company's origins. Managers should avoid any unnecessary comparisons that might reflect the home country management's belief that the host country might be inferior in some way to the home country. It is often possible – sometimes even desirable – to compare products, but it is not prudent to publicly compare governments, labor, or technology.

It may be wise to hire most, if not all, top-level managers of the foreign subsidiary from the available host country management pool. Not only will these individuals project a more local image, but they usually understand local problems well and can often help the company avoid blunders.

PROMOTION

Many companies have encountered serious problems trying to coordinate their sales efforts. All plans should be in writing, and it is advisable to charge someone with the responsibility of central coordination. Thus, risks are lessened and money saving opportunities may arise. Coca-Cola, for instance, requires that all overseas marketing plans be submitted to the central office well before they are instituted. This allows the company time to examine the concepts. The firm's experiences with similar plans can be reviewed and necessary changes can be made. Sometimes central company managers discover that similar plans have failed in other overseas ventures or sometimes they determine that similar plans have succeeded. There is no need to reinvent the wheel. Coordination not only reduces the possibility of errors, it also provides a company with the opportunity to fine-tune its promotions.

Dozens of blunders have been made by firms that failed to carefully investigate the local customs and preferences of their potential customers. Since social norms vary so greatly from country to country, it is extremely difficult for any outsider to be knowledgeable of them all. As pointed out previously, local input can be vital. Many promotional errors could have been averted had this warning been heeded.

TRANSLATION

Advertising is a tricky business. More mistakes seem to have been made in advertising than in any other business task, and these errors have most often been due to faulty translations. It is usually recommended that the translation of an advertisement stress the ad's general theme and concept rather than precisely duplicate the original slogan.

There are several methods known that can help a company avert potential translation disasters. Certainly a company may hire an exceptionally brilliant translator, but certain types of errors can still surface. The translator may enjoy an extraordinary gift for the language or have studied in the foreign country but may be unfamiliar with many idiomatic expressions and slang. Therefore, in many cases it is wise to also hire a second translator, one familiar with the local slang and unusual idioms, to "backtranslate."

Backtranslation is one of the best techniques available to reduce translation errors. Backtranslation requires that one individual translate the message into the desired foreign language and that another party translate the foreign version back into the original language. Thus, a company can determine if its intended message is actually being presented. An Australian soft drink company discovered the value of backtranslation during the planning stages of its entry into the Hong Kong market. The company had hoped to employ its successful slogan "Baby, it's cold inside," but before using the translated version of the slogan, the firm had it translated back into English. This proved to be a wise move. The message backtranslated to "Small mosquito, on the inside it is very cold." "Small mosquito," a local colloquial expression for a small child, simply did not convey the same thing as the friendly English slang word *baby* for "woman." The intended message would have been lost had the original translated version been used.

The use of backtranslation uncovers many translation errors but can be frustrating if performed by mediocre translators. Naturally, the better the translator is, the fewer the problems encountered. The difficulty, therefore, lies in determining the ability of a potential translator. One slow and expensive method is to allow the translator a trial run. This method will expose any problems, but it then becomes necessary to determine if the errors were committed by the original translator or by the person translating back to the first language.

Firms requiring major or important translation work should thoroughly investigate any potential translator. The following points should be covered during the candidate's interview.

1. Does the translator maintain or have access to a library or reference books dealing with the appropriate subject and industry?

2. Does the translator understand the required technical terms? Does the translator know the foreign words for these specialized terms? If not, how are they to be learned?

3. Does the translator have a staff or access to experts in various fields (i.e., law)?

4. Will someone check the work? If so, what are the credentials of the assistant? (It is often advisable to request references and copies of material that has been translated for other clients.)

5. How recently has the translator been to the country involved? (Sometimes it is necessary to determine how current the translator's knowledge is. Because languages do change, especially slang, it is not enough to hire someone familiar with the foreign language and culture. Even a native tends to lose track of slang and idioms after being away from home for a few years.)

Once a translator has been chosen, there are several things that a company can do to facilitate the job. For instance, since it has often taken the company many months to develop the promotional materials, a translator should not be asked to translate the material hurriedly. Given adequate time, a much better translation is likely to result. A simple literal translation is not generally appropriate, so a translator may need time to be creative.

Of course, this is not to say that the translator should not be given a deadline. It is important to tell the person when the material must be finished and inform him or her of the timing of its expected use. On occasion, a manager has failed to inform the translator of the season in which the ad is to run, and the translator has assumed an inappropriate time period. A company does little to enhance its image when it runs a winter advertisement in the summer. (A few companies have also blundered by promoting advertisements during ill-suited seasons when they simply forgot that the Southern Hemisphere has the opposite seasons of the Northern Hemisphere.)

Naturally, it is important for the translator to understand the type of media to be used and the general characteristics of the audience. This allows the person to determine the proper level of formality and the correct tone. A translator must be given the freedom to modify original wording. As discussed previously, literal translations can prove disastrous. Likewise, because the translated version of a message may require more words than the original, it is not wise to limit the translator to a particular amount of time or space. Doing so may seriously jeopardize the effectiveness of the message.

If possible, firms are advised to reduce the use of overly technical terms and to avoid industry jargon in their promotional materials. It is also advisable to limit the use of large numbers. Any number over 10,000 may be easily mistranslated. The number "one billion," for example, is numerically written with nine zeroes in the United States but with twelve zeroes in Europe.

Since humor is also almost impossible to translate, it is best to avoid using jokes in advertising. What is regarded as funny by some is often not considered so by others.

Finally, a translator should be provided with as much relevant information as possible and should be informed of both the message's objectives and what is essential to the theme. By allowing the translator to examine previous company translations as well as translated slogans of competing companies, the individual will not only assure that any key phrase associated with the company is included but will avoid accidentally using any competitor's phrases.

To reduce translation needs and overcome communication difficulties in countries that experience high levels of illiteracy, visual methods of communication are sometimes used. Libby, for instance, has successfully promoted its products through inexpensive commercials that feature a clown enjoying Libby products. In these ads, no words are spoken.

Using English in Non-English-speaking Countries
Sometimes companies have found that the best solution to the translation problem is simply to not translate the material. If the locals can understand English or if they simply do not need to comprehend the message, then it may be safer for a firm from an English-speaking country to stick with its English copy. The use of translators is always risky because they are putting words into the company's mouth. A firm does not need for them to put a foot in there also.

To reduce the problems that may occur when English is used in a non-English-speaking country:

1. Keep the entire message short and simple, including words and sentences.

2. Avoid jargon or slang.

3. Avoid idioms.

4. Avoid humor if possible.

5. Use appropriate currencies and measurements.

6. Cite examples if feasible.

7. Repeat important points.

If a company decides to go ahead with an English message through a verbal advertisement directed to an audience whose native language is not English, the speaker should speak slowly, speak carefully, correctly pronounce all words, and pause between sentences.

As it is very likely that during some part of the overseas venture someone from the company will engage in a conversation in English with an individual who has some difficulty understanding English, the following guidelines should be observed:

1. Time should be allowed for questions and discussions.

2. Patience is important; permit the individual to find the words to respond.

3. Questions should be asked to determine if the message has been comprehended.

4. The individual should be complimented and reassured of his or her ability to speak English.

5. Express gratefulness that the individual is speaking English.

6. Express regret that the conversation could not have been spoken in the other person's language.

(It should be noted, however, that speaking a few polite, social words in the foreign language is appreciated and highly recommended.)

Ideally, company literature and material should be provided prior to the conversation. This allows the other individual a chance to prepare and should greatly increase the person's comprehension. After the discussion, the person should be sent a summary of the conversation. This also will increase the likelihood that the conversation was correctly understood.

During World War II, the phrase "Loose lips sink ships" was used to discourage people from talking about military matters when they were within the hearing range of strangers. For international businesses, the phrase might be appropriately modified to "Misunderstood lips sink companies." Multinational firms will encounter enough unavoidable and unpredictable problems. They need not make avoidable blunders as well.

MARKET RESEARCH

The use of properly conducted market research could have reduced or eliminated most international business blunders. Market researchers have the ability to uncover adaptation needs, potential name problems, promotional requirements, and proper market strategies. Even many of the translation blunders could have been avoided if sound research techniques had been used.

A number of the cited blunders occurred because firms tried to use the same product, name, promotional material, or strategy overseas that they used at home. They were hoping that what worked well at home would also work well abroad. Although this is understandable, it is nevertheless often unrealistic. Standardization promotes certain efficiencies, but in many instances it is not a worthwhile strategy to pursue. Limitations do exist, and it is important for firms to recognize and understand this.

The use of market research enables a firm to determine its limits of standardization. The research serves two major functions: It can help a company identify what the firm can hope to accomplish, and it can help a company realize what the firm should not do. Neither consideration should be overlooked.

Few would question the value of marketing research as part of international business planning. Unfortunately, it is not an easy undertaking and is extremely complicated. Even the smallest of details must not be ignored during analysis. The data required varies with the firm, its products, and the decisions being made. Research helps a company determine whether or not to go abroad, which countries to enter, how to enter the foreign markets, and which marketing strategies to use.

CONCLUSION

This collection of international business blunders was not gathered with the intention of using it to poke fun at multinational companies or to make them appear inept. Rather, it was assembled to provide valuable, vicarious examples of business practices that should be avoided. The blunders others have experienced provide us with interesting lessons – ones surely preferable to learning through experience.

In reality, companies are generally quite competent. Considering the many ways a firm can blunder, it must be doing most things correctly just to survive. This thought was best expressed by a senior executive from General Motors when he was asked to verify one of the problems reported in this book. He replied that although GM may have made a few errors overseas, when that very small number is compared to the many decisions made by GM, it is "a good batting average." This is true. Most firms make few serious mistakes and even fewer avoidable blunders. If they did, they simply would not be in business long. Although numerous errors have been reported here, one must realize that the mistakes have been made by many different companies over a number of years.

The fact that firms make these mistakes should not be all that surprising anyway. After all, it is not really a company that blunders, but its employees. Employees are only human, and we all make mistakes. Sometimes our errors are personal, but sometimes they are made on behalf of corporations.

It should also be noted that the blunders reported may not be totally accurate. Although most of the anecdotes have been reported in the media and efforts were made to verify them, verification has not been easy. Many corporations have been reluctant to respond to inquiries. Several firms have replied with a version of "We are sorry but we cannot provide you with the information about that possible event. The person who had been responsible for that area is *no longer with the company*." These statements possibly bear an added message: If one wants to remain with a firm, avoid making blunders.

Since firms do not appreciate appearing foolish, they sometimes deny a witnessed event. But as the public becomes more and more aware that all firms have made some mistakes, these denials become less necessary. There are cases, however, where reports of company blunders have proven to be false. The wrong companies have been identified or the entire story has been fictionalized. This author discovered an excellent example of a false report when trying to verify a story regarding Exxon's ventures in Thailand. The report stated that Exxon's ad "Put a tiger in your tank" failed in Thailand because the tiger does not represent power and strength there. However, a series of letters and investigations in both Asia and the United States revealed what had really happened. Overzealous competitors had deliberately planted the false story hoping that the U.S. media would pick it up. In fact, not only is the tiger a symbol of strength in Thailand, Exxon continued to use the ad effectively and was able to capture a large share of the local market.

Unfortunately, this book may also contain a few errors. Naturally, any error is greatly regretted. There certainly have been errors of omission since this book does not cite or report every blunder ever committed in international business.

One final word of warning: No one should be under the illusion that all blunders have been committed; others are likely to occur in the future. The more we learn of past blunders, the more we will understand them and their causes and the better we can prepare ourselves to avoid future blunders. Hopefully, this book will help reduce the number of blunders made. We do not want readers' future decisions to end up being reported in the next edition of this book!

NOTES

Chapter 1

1. More information on this and similar incidents is reported by Edward T. Hall in *The Silent Language* (New York: Doubleday, 1959).
2. The problems of international gift giving are discussed in a 32-page booklet by Kathleen Reardon, *International Business Gift-Giving Customs* (Parker Pen Company, P.O. Box 5100, Janesville, Wisconsin, 53547).

Chapter 2

3. Many versions of this event exist. Most historians, however, currently seem to believe that the bullets encased in pig wax represented the "final straw." Basically, the bullets provided an example of the degree of British insensitivity to Indian cultural values and needs. In reality, the East India Company needed to modify its entire operation.

Chapter 3

4. For further details, see Carolyn Pfaff, "Champagne Cigs Cause Headache," *Advertising Age*, 30 March 1981, p. 2.

Chapter 5

5. Although many people have cited the "pregnancy" problem experienced by Parker Pen, they seldom provide any details. The author, therefore, thanks the Parker Pen Company management for its open and refreshingly frank discussion of this past event and its causes. All firms have at one time or another made mistakes. If more firms were as helpful as the Parker Pen Company, then we would more clearly understand the underlying causes of these errors and avoid them in the future.
6. It should be noted that the company denies that it experienced these translation difficulties in Germany but does admit that the ad was misunderstood in Asia. Indeed, the phrase "Come alive with Pepsi"

must have created a real challenge for translators in many parts of the world. If the company encountered problems in only one or two countries, it should consider itself quite fortunate.

7. This list was adapted from Maurice Brisebois, "Industrial Advertising and Marketing in Quebec," *The Marketer*, Spring–Summer 1966, p. 10.

8. "Translating Can Be Beastly," *Spectrum Newsletter*, Spring 1981, p. 2.

Chapter 7

9. "Golden Touches Turned to Lead," *Time*, 30 November 1981, p. 66.

10. Massey-Ferguson claims that the problems were not predictable and caused primarily by the Turkish government. Outside reports, however, lay more of the blame on management. See, for example, "Turkey Cancels Plans for Tractor Output by Massey-Ferguson," *The Wall Street Journal*, 18 November 1970, p. 27.

Chapter 8

11. The complaint voiced by Colgate-Palmolive dealt with the possibility of consumers mistaking the two products. Although many firms face competition from counterfeit products, Unilever argued that it was not attempting any such strategy. However, Australian courts ruled that the resemblance was too great. For details, read Len Blanket, "Aussie Court Bans Package Ad," *Advertising Age*, 12 October 1981, p. 72.

BIBLIOGRAPHY

Aman, Reinhold. "New, Improved Dreck! Interlingual Taboo in Personal Names, Brand Names, and Language Learning." *Maledicta*, Winter 1979, pp. 145–52.

Armao, Rosemary. "Worst Blunders: Firms Laugh through Tears." *American Business*, January 1981, p. 12.

Arpan, J. S., D. A. Ricks, and D. J. Patton. "The Meaning of Miscues Made by Multinationals." *Management International Review* 4–5, 1974, pp. 3–16.

Axtell, Roger E. *Do's and Taboos Around the World.* New York: John Wiley and Sons, 1985.

Axtell, Roger E. *The Do's and Taboos of International Trade.* New York: John Wiley and Sons, 1989.

Black, Gilbert J. "Tighten Your Overseas Marketing Plan." *Sales Marketing Today*, August–September 1969.

Blanket, Len. "Aussie Court Bans Package Ad." *Advertising Age*, 12 October 1981, p. 72.

Bowen, F. A. "Ad Bloopers Abroad-Amusing and Sometimes Costly." *F. A. Bowen Reports*, Janesville, WI.

Brisebois, Maurice. "Industrial Advertising and Marketing in Quebec," *The Marketer*, Spring–Summer 1966, p. 10.

Brislin, Richard W. *Cross-Cultural Encounters: Face-to-Face Interaction.* New York: Pergamon Press, 1981.

Buzzell, Robert D. "Can You Standardize Multinational Marketing?" *Harvard Business Review*, November–December 1968, pp. 102–13.

Copeland, Lennie, and Lewis Griggs. *Going International: How To Make Friends and Deal Effectively in the Global Marketplace.* New York: Random House, 1985.

"Corporate-Size Blunders Provide Laughs and Lessons." *Chicago Tribune*, 28 December 1980, section 5, p. 6.

Frost, David, and Michael Deakin. *David Frost's Book of the World's Worst Decisions*. New York: Crown Publishers, 1983.

Galante, Steven P. "How Foreigners Botch Their U.S. Investments," *The Wall Street Journal*, 6 June 1984.

Glover, M. Katherine. "Do's and Taboos: Cultural Aspects of International Business." *Business America*, 13 August 1990, pp. 2–6.

Goldberg, M. Hirsh. *The Blunder Book*. New York: William Morrow & Company, 1985.

"Golden Touches Turned to Lead," *Time*, 30 November 1981, p. 66.

Halborg, Al. "How to Use Names." *Management Today*, November 1979, pp. 113–16.

Hall, Edward T. *Beyond Culture*. Garden City, NY: Anchor Press/Doubleday, 1976.

Hall, Edward T. *The Silent Language*. New York: Doubleday, 1959.

Hall, Edward T. "The Silent Language in Overseas Business." *Harvard Business Review*, May–June 1960, pp. 87–96.

Hall, Edward T., and Mildred Reed Hall. *Understanding Cultural Differences: Germans, French, and Americans*. Yarmouth, ME: Intercultural Press, 1990.

Harris, Philip R., and Robert T. Moran. *Managing Cultural Differences*. Houston, TX: Gulf Publishing Co., 1987.

Hill, G. Christian. "More Firms Turn to Translation Experts to Avoid Costly, Embarrassing Mistakes." *The Wall Street Journal*, 13 January 1977, p. 34.

"How Ads Were Changed to Reach Minorities." *Advertising Age*, 7 April 1980, p. 5.

"Interpreter de Riguer for Marketing Abroad." *American Business*, November 1979, p. 23.

League, Frederick A. "Why Companies Fail Abroad." *Columbia Journal of World Business*, July–August 1968, p. 55.

Lee, James A. "Cultural Analysis in Overseas Operations." *Harvard Business Review*, March–April 1966, pp. 106–14.

Manville, Richard. "33 Caveats for the Prospective Overseas Marketer." *Marketing News*, 10 March 1978, pp. 6–7.

Mauser, Ferdinand F. "Losing Something in Translation." *Harvard Business Review*, July–August 1977, pp. 5–6.

Mayer, Charles S. "The Lessons of Multinational Marketing Research." *Business Horizons*, November–December 1978, pp. 7–13.

Pfaff, Carolyn. "Champagne Cigs Cause Headache," *Advertising Age*, 30 March 1981, p. 2.

Reardon, Kathleen. *International Business Gift-Giving Customs: A Guide for American Executives.* Janesville, WI: The Parker Pen Company, 1981.

Ricks, David A. *Big Business Blunders.* Homewood, IL: Richard D. Irwin, 1983.

Ricks, David A. "Products That Crashed into the Language Barrier." *Business and Society Review,* Spring 1983, pp. 46-49.

Ricks, David A. "How to Avoid Business Blunders Abroad." *Business,* April–June 1984, pp. 3–11.

Ricks, David A. "International Business Blunders: An Update." *Business and Economic Review,* January–March 1988, pp. 11–14.

Ricks, David A., Jeffrey S. Arpan, and Marilyn Y. C. Fu. "Pitfalls in Advertising Overseas." *Journal of Advertising Research,* December 1974, pp. 47-51.

Ricks, David A., Marilyn Y. C. Fu, and Jeffrey S. Arpan. *International Business Blunders.* Columbus, OH: Grid, 1974.

Ricks, David A., and Vijay Mahajan. "Blunders in International Marketing: Fact or Fiction." *Long Range Planning,* February 1984, pp. 78–83.

Rossman, Marlene L. *The International Businesswoman: A Guide to Success in the Global Marketplace.* New York, NY: Praeger Publishers, 1986.

Rotbart, Dean. "To Make Mr. Ricks' List, a Company Must Commit a Major Blunder Abroad." *The Wall Street Journal,* 13 March 1981, p. 21.

"The Spanish-American Business Wars." *Worldwide P & I Planning,* May–June 1971, pp. 30–40.

Stewart, Thomas A. "Lessons From U.S. Business Blunders." *Fortune,* 23 April 1990, pp. 128–141.

Stridsberg, Albert. "U.S. Advertisers Win Some, Lose Some in Foreign Market." *Advertising Age,* 6 May 1974, p. 18.

Terpstra, Vern, and Kenneth David. *The Cultural Environment of International Business,* 2d ed. Cincinnati, OH: South-Western Publishing, 1985.

Tharp, David. "U.S. Marketing 'No Go' in Japan." *Advertising Age,* 11 December 1978, p. 164.

Train, John. "Costly Imbroglios." *Forbes,* 20 July 1981, pp. 120–21.

"Translating Can Be Beastly." *Spectrum Newsletter,* Spring 1981, p. 2.

"Turkey Cancels Plans for Tractor Output by Massey-Ferguson." *The Wall Street Journal,* 18 November 1970, p. 27.

Winick, Charles. "Anthropology's Contributions to Marketing." *Journal of Marketing,* July 1961, pp. 53–60.

Winkworth, Stephen. *Great Commercial Disasters.* London: Macmillan London Limited, 1980.

Yoshino, Michael Y. "So You're Setting Up Shop in Asia." *Columbia Journal of World Business*, November–December 1967, pp. 61–66.

INDEX OF COMPANIES

INDEX OF COUNTRIES

INDEX OF PRODUCTS